I0410342

CONTENTS

Protecting America/Global War On Terror 1

Freedom Agenda 6

Military Transformation 9

Veterans 11

Defense Against Weapons of Mass Destruction 12

Global Health Initiatives 15

Tax Relief 17

Trade 19

No Child Left Behind 20

Health Care 23

Medicare 25

Faith-Based and Community Initiatives 27

USA Freedom Corps 29

Energy and Climate Change 31

Conservation and the Environment 34

Stem Cell Research 36

Judicial Appointments 38

First Lady Laura Bush 39

President Bush Has Kept America Safe

President Bush Fundamentally Reshaped Our Strategy To Protect The American People

"Because of ... the efforts of many across all levels of government, we have not suffered another attack on our soil since September the 11th, 2001."

– President George W. Bush, 3/8/08

Following the attacks of September 11, 2001, President Bush took the fight to the enemy to defeat the terrorists and protect America. The President deployed all elements of national power to combat terrorism, which had previously been considered primarily a "law enforcement" issue. He transformed our military and strengthened our national security institutions to wage the War on Terror and secure our homeland. The President also made missile defense operational and advanced counterproliferation efforts to help prevent our enemies from threatening us, and our allies, with weapons of mass destruction.

Secured the Homeland

- Protected our Nation and prevented another attack on U.S. soil for more than seven years, modernized our national security institutions and tools of war, and bolstered our homeland security. Under the President's watch, numerous terrorist attacks have been prevented in the United States. These include:
    - An attempt to bomb fuel tanks at JFK airport;
    - A plot to blow up airliners bound for the East Coast;
    - A plan to destroy the tallest skyscraper in Los Angeles;
    - A plot by six al Qaeda inspired individuals to kill soldiers at Fort Dix Army Base in New Jersey;
    - A plan to attack a Chicago-area shopping mall using grenades; and
    - A plot to attack the Sears Tower in Chicago.
- Arrested and convicted more than two dozen terrorists and their supporters in America since 9/11.
- Froze the financial assets in the United States of hundreds of individuals and entities linked to terrorism and proliferation.
- Doubled the Border Patrol to more than 18,000 agents, equipped the Border Patrol with better technology and new infrastructure, and effectively ended the process of catch and release at the border. Increased border security and immigration enforcement funding by more than 160 percent and constructed hundreds of miles of fencing and vehicle barriers.
- Instituted a process to screen every commercial air passenger in the country, launched credentialing initiatives to better identify passengers, and expanded the Federal Air Marshal Program. Replaced the multiple watchlists that were in place prior to 9/11 with a single, consolidated watchlist, and incorporated biometrics in screening and identifying individuals entering our country. Created US-VISIT to screen foreign travelers and prevent terrorists from entering America. Required secure identification at our ports of entry to better monitor individuals entering the United States.
- Invested more than $38 billion in public health and medical systems, created a biothreat air monitoring system, and developed a national strategy and international partnership on avian and pandemic flu.

Waged the Global War on Terror

- Removed the Taliban from power and brought freedom to the 25 million people of Afghanistan.
- Freed 25 million Iraqis from the rule of Saddam Hussein, a dictator who murdered his own people, invaded his neighbors, and repeatedly defied United Nations resolutions.
- Captured or killed hundreds of al Qaeda leaders and operatives in more than two dozen countries with the help of partner nations. September 11 mastermind Khalid Sheikh Mohammed is in U.S. custody and Abu Musab al-Zarqawi, the former leader of al-Qaeda in Iraq, was killed in 2006. Removed al Qaeda's safe-haven in Afghanistan and crippled al Qaeda in Iraq, including defeating al Qaeda in its former stronghold of Anbar Province.

Transformed Our Approach to Combating Terrorism After the 9/11 Attacks

- Increased the size of our ground forces and number of unmanned aerial vehicles and strengthened special operations forces by increasing resources, manpower, and capabilities. Increased the Defense Department's base budget more than 70 percent since 2001, including increased funding for military pay and benefits, research, and development. Started moving American forces from Cold War garrisons in Europe and Asia so they can deploy more quickly to any region of the world. Modernized and transformed the National Guard from a strategic reserve to an operational reserve.
- Forged a new, comprehensive cybersecurity policy to improve the security of Federal government and military computer systems and made protecting these systems a national priority.
- Improved cargo screening and security at U.S. ports and increased containerized cargo screening overseas.
- Established a more unified, collaborative intelligence community under the leadership of a Director of National Intelligence to ensure information is shared among intelligence and law enforcement professionals so they have the information they need to protect the American people while respecting the legal rights of all U.S. persons, including freedoms, civil liberties, and privacy rights guaranteed by Federal law.
- Consolidated 22 agencies and 180,000 employees under a new agency, the Department of Homeland Security, to foster a comprehensive, coordinated approach to protecting our country.
- Advocated for and signed into law the USA PATRIOT Act, the Intelligence Reform and Terrorism Prevention Act, and a modernization of the Foreign Intelligence Surveillance Act.
- Shifted the FBI's focus from investigating terrorist attacks to preventing them. Created the National Security Branch at the FBI, which combines the FBI's counterterrorism, counterintelligence, intelligence, and weapons of mass destruction (WMD) elements under the leadership of a senior FBI official.
- Created the Terrorist Screening Center and the National Security Division at the Department of Justice.

Invigorated International Alliances And Partnerships To Make America Safer And More Secure

- Partnered with nations in Europe, the Middle East, Asia, Africa, and the Western Hemisphere on intelligence sharing and law enforcement coordination to break up terrorist networks and bring terrorists to justice.
- Transformed NATO to face 21st century threats, including strengthening the Alliance's capabilities against WMD and cyber attacks, while leading the international military effort in Afghanistan.
- Established the Proliferation Security Initiative (PSI) and other multilateral coalitions to stop WMD proliferation and strengthen our ability to locate and secure nuclear and radiological materials around the world. Dismantled and prevented the reconstitution of the A.Q. Khan proliferation network, an extensive, international network that had spread sensitive nuclear technology and capability to Iran, Libya, and North Korea.
- Worked with European partners to limit Iran's ability to develop weapons of mass destruction and ballistic missiles and finance terrorism, and initiated targeted sanctions against Iran's Quds Force. Gathered support for and won passage of three Chapter VII United Nations Security Council resolutions that impose sanctions on Iran and require it to suspend its uranium enrichment and other proliferation-sensitive nuclear activities.
- Established the Six Party Talks framework in partnership with China, South Korea, Japan, and Russia. Obtained a commitment from North Korea to abandon all nuclear weapons and existing nuclear programs. Since November 2007, USG experts have supervised North Korea's activities to disable its plutonium production capability.
- Persuaded Libya to disclose and dismantle all aspects of its WMD and advanced missile programs, renounce terrorism, and accept responsibility for prior acts of terror. Normalized our relations with Libya as a result.
- Signed agreements for missile defense sites in the Czech Republic and Poland to help protect America and its allies from the threat of WMD delivered by ballistic missiles. Obtained NATO endorsement of plans to deploy missile defense assets in Europe.

Global War On Terror

President Bush Has Kept Our Nation Safe In The Seven Years Following 9/11

Following the attacks of September 11, 2001, President Bush recognized the threat posed by terrorists and took action to protect Americans and defeat violent extremism. Because of the actions taken by President Bush, America is safer, more secure, and winning the War on Terror. Seven years later:

- 50 million people have been liberated, and two totalitarian regimes have been removed;
- The al Qaeda network has been weakened;
- We have not experienced another attack on American soil;
- Our military has been transformed to meet the challenges of the 21st century;
- We have expanded our intelligence capabilities to confront today's enemy; and
- We have created new and essential institutions needed to wage the War on Terror, including the Department of Homeland Security and Office of the Director of National Intelligence.

We Have Been On The Offense Against Our Enemies Since The 9/11 Attacks

President Bush has kept us safe by weakening al Qaeda and its affiliates. Hundreds of al Qaeda leaders and operatives have been captured or killed, including 9/11 mastermind Khalid Sheikh Mohammad, who is currently awaiting trial by a Military Commission. The United States also apprehended several leading figures in the al Qaeda East Africa network through intelligence sharing and military action.

Since 9/11, more than two dozen terrorists and supporters have been convicted in the United States of terrorism-related crimes. Several key financiers and facilitators of terrorism have been isolated and captured, while more than 400 individuals and entities have had their assets frozen and isolated from the U.S. financial system.

President Bush took the fight to violent extremists in Iraq and Afghanistan and across the world so that we do not have to fight them on American soil. The United States and its coalition partners removed al Qaeda's safe haven in Afghanistan and al Qaeda is on the run in Iraq, including in its former stronghold of Anbar Province. The United States also acted to prevent al Qaeda safe havens from emerging in the Horn of Africa and Southeast Asia.

There have been no attacks on American soil since 9/11, and the United States and our allies have disrupted key terrorist plots around the world. The President has built a 90-nation coalition to fight terrorism. The United States has partnered with nations in Europe, the Middle East, Asia, Africa, and Latin America on intelligence sharing and law enforcement coordination to break up terrorist networks and bring terrorists to justice. Some of our counterterrorism victories include the following:

- **September 2007:** German authorities disrupted a terrorist cell that was planning attacks on military installations and facilities used by Americans in Germany. The Germans arrested three suspected members of the Islamic Jihad Union, a group that has links to al Qaeda and supports al Qaeda's global jihadist agenda.
- **September 2007:** Danish authorities disrupted a cell, which included an al Qaeda-trained individual, planning terrorist attacks using explosives.
- **June 2007:** Four individuals were charged with plotting to blow up major fuel tanks at JFK Airport. Three of the individuals have been arrested, and the United States is pursuing extradition of the fourth.
- **May 2007:** The FBI arrested six al Qaeda-inspired individuals plotting to kill soldiers at Fort Dix Army Base in New Jersey. The plotters purchased weapons for the attack, which they had been planning since January 2006.
- **August 2006:** British authorities disrupted a plot to blow up passenger airplanes flying from the UK to the United States.

➤ **The United States supported the creation of a democratic Afghan government and fostered broad international support for Afghanistan through NATO and the U.N.** Afghanistan has ratified a new democratic Constitution with strong protections for women's rights and civil liberties; held the country's first Presidential election; and held the first free and fair legislative elections since 1969. Today, six million Afghans are attending school, and 85 percent of Afghans have access to basic health care. The United States has committed over $10 billion in 2008 and 2009 for political and economic development. The Afghan government is preparing for the next round of elections in 2009 with U.S. and international assistance.

➤ **Iraq is now a young democracy and an ally in fighting terrorists.** The President's decision to send an additional 30,000 soldiers and Marines into Iraq as part of the "surge" has resulted in improved security conditions that have opened up space for political and economic advances. Iraq has seen meaningful progress, but this progress is fragile and there will be challenging times ahead. This success has fostered the appropriate conditions for Iraqi authorities to take the lead in all security operations for Anbar province.

➤ **President Bush persuaded Libya to dismantle its Weapons of Mass Destruction (WMD) programs and renounce terrorism, leading to a normalization of our relationship with Libya.** Just last week, Secretary of State Condoleezza Rice made a historic visit to Libya, making her the highest ranking U.S. official to visit the country since 1957.

➤ **The President worked with the international community to isolate the regime in Tehran, and won support for three U.N. Security Council resolutions imposing sanctions on Iran because of its failure to suspend its uranium enrichment and other proliferation sensitive activities.**

President Bush has teamed with international partners to prevent the proliferation of WMDs. We have expanded international efforts to deny terrorists access to advanced conventional weaponry and to WMDs, their delivery systems, and related materials.

President Bush Has Transformed The Institutions And Tools To Fight Terror And Protect America

The President worked with Congress to implement reforms and create the institutions needed to wage the War on Terror. The President also integrated and unified intelligence gathering; disrupted terrorist financing; and created new legal and law enforcement frameworks to combat terrorism and deny safe haven to terrorist groups. The President:

➤ **Transformed the United States military to meet the challenges of the 21st century.** President Bush provided our military with the tools, equipment, and resources to combat terrorism and other new challenges. We started moving American forces from Cold War garrisons in Europe and Asia so they can deploy more quickly to any region of the world to confront emerging threats.

➤ **Strengthened our ability to protect the American people by directing the most extensive security reorganization of the Federal Government since 1947.** President Bush and his Administration have enhanced our homeland security and counterterrorism infrastructure through the creation of the Department of Homeland Security (DHS), the Office of the Director of National Intelligence (ODNI), the National Counterterrorism Center (NCTC), the Terrorist Screening Center (TSC), the Homeland Security Council (HSC), and U.S. Northern Command, a Department of Defense combatant command focused on homeland defense and civil support.
   - **DHS** consolidated 22 Federal entities and 180,000 employees under one roof to foster a comprehensive, coordinated approach to protecting the U.S. homeland. DHS and FBI, in partnership with Federal, State, and local authorities, created a national network of 66 fusion centers in 48 states to facilitate information sharing on terrorist threats and operational planning.
   - The **NCTC** leads our Nation's effort to combat terrorism at home and abroad by analyzing the threat, sharing that information with our partners, and integrating all instruments of national power to ensure unity of effort.

- The **ODNI** coordinates and integrates and leads the work of the Intelligence Community as a unified enterprise, led by the Director of National Intelligence (DNI), to ensure information is shared among intelligence and law enforcement professionals.
- The **TSC** maintains the Government's consolidated list of suspected terrorists and individuals with terrorist links and helps get this information into the hands of State and local law enforcement.
- **HSC** ensures coordination of all homeland security-related activities among executive departments and agencies and promotes the effective development and implementation of homeland security policies.

➤ **Modernized the Foreign Intelligence Surveillance Act to provide the tools needed to win the War on Terror and protect America from another attack.** This vital legislation allows our law enforcement and intelligence professionals as well as future administrations with the ability to quickly and effectively monitor the plans of terrorists outside the United States, while respecting the privacy and liberties of the American people.

➤ **Strengthened our defenses to protect the American people by implementing the recommendations of the 9/11 Commission.** Together with Congress, the President restructured and reformed the Federal government to focus resources on counterterrorism and took the necessary steps to improve the Nation's homeland security.

The President Has Implemented Programs To Secure Our Homeland And Fight The War On Terror

The President and his Administration have increased border and transportation security. President Bush is implementing an effective system of layered defense by strengthening the screening of people and goods overseas and by tracking and disrupting the international travel of terrorists. The President:

➤ **Created the Transportation Security Administration (TSA).** TSA instituted a process to screen every commercial air passenger in the country, launched credentialing initiatives to strengthen our ability to identify passengers, and expanded the Federal Air Marshal program. We have hardened cockpit doors, armed pilots to defend the flight deck, and strengthened air cargo security.

➤ **Enhanced U.S. port security and increased scanning for radiological and nuclear threats.** The President coordinated Federal, State, local, and industry port partners through the establishment of formalized Area Maritime Security Committees and Plans that clarify roles and responsibilities. Today, more than 98 percent of all containers entering the supply chain via U.S. seaports are scanned for potential radiological and nuclear threats – prior to 9/11, zero percent were scanned.

➤ **Increased containerized cargo screening overseas.** We have worked with our international partners to employ the Container Security Initiative in 58 foreign seaports, screening 86 percent of all U.S.-destined containerized cargo being screened overseas before it enters the U.S. supply chain.

➤ **Increased border security and interior enforcement funding more than 110 percent and equipped the Border Patrol with better technology and new infrastructure.** We have also added more than 8,000 border patrol agents. The Administration has constructed hundreds of miles of fencing and vehicle barriers along America's southern border and is moving toward the goal of 670 miles by the end of the year.

President Bush's Freedom Agenda Helped Protect The American People

President Bush Has Advanced Liberty And Democracy As The Great Alternatives To Repression And Radicalism

President Bush has kept his pledge to strengthen democracy and promote peace around the world. In his Second Inaugural Address, President Bush pledged America to the ultimate goal of ending tyranny in the world. He has promoted the spread of freedom as the great alternative to the terrorists' ideology of hatred, because expanding liberty and democracy will help defeat extremism and protect the American people. President Bush also acted quickly and decisively to help end international crises that arose during his term in office and to confront regimes that threatened our Nation and world security. By working to spread liberty in these volatile regions and combating the conditions that can breed extremism, the President has helped make the American people safer.

The President's Freedom Agenda Helped Emerging Democracies Build The Institutions That Sustain Liberty

Under President Bush's leadership, the United States and its partners freed 25 million Iraqis from the rule of Saddam Hussein, a dictator who murdered his own people, invaded his neighbors, and repeatedly defied United Nations resolutions. The Administration supported the creation of a freely elected Iraqi government that is operating under one of the most progressive constitutions in the Arab world and helped train and equip more than half a million Iraqi Army and police forces. U.S. and Iraqi forces have made significant progress in reducing sectarian violence, restoring basic security to Iraqi communities, and driving terrorists and illegal militias out of their safe havens. Iraqi Security Forces are now responsible for security in 13 of 18 provinces (including al-Qaeda in Iraq's former stronghold of Anbar Province), and this increase in security has helped clear the way for political and economic development. Iraq's parliament passed important laws on provincial powers, amnesty, and elections and also approved new strategic agreements with the United States. Iraq's economy will increasingly diversify, rely on private investment, and stand on its own. In their 2008 budget, Iraqi funding for reconstruction exceeded U.S. funding by more than ten to one, and American spending for large-scale reconstruction projects is approaching zero. The Iraqi people are looking forward to a new round of provincial elections in January and national elections later in 2009. The Administration successfully negotiated a Strategic Framework Agreement and a Security Agreement with Iraq, which will further strengthen the relationship between our nations, provide the United States with vital protections and authorities to continue our mission to help stabilize Iraq, and establish a path for U.S. forces to reduce their presence in Iraq and return home on success.

President Bush helped establish an emerging democratic Afghan government and helped improve the lives of the Afghan people, especially women and children. Together, we worked to ensure a stable and safe environment to allow gains in local governance and economic development to be sustained. Thanks to the courage of the Afghan people and their international partners, a nation that was once a safe haven for al Qaeda is now an emerging democracy, and we are committed to its development and stability. More than six million children, approximately two million of whom are girls, are now in Afghan schools, compared to fewer than one million in 2001. In 2002, Presidents Bush and Karzai launched the US-Afghan Women's Council. Mrs. Bush is Honorary Chair of the Council, a public-private partnership that supports Afghan women in the areas of political and economic participation, literacy, and education, as well as legal awareness and access to health care.

President Bush generated international pressure to end the Syrian occupation of Lebanon and helped promote democracy and restore civilian rule in Pakistan. He strengthened our relationship with and support to a democratic Lebanon and called for parliamentary elections in Pakistan that reflected the will of the people and ended more than eight years of military rule.

President Bush laid the groundwork for a future Israeli-Palestinian peace agreement and a democratic Palestinian state by launching direct negotiations between Israel and the Palestinian Authority (PA) at the Annapolis Conference and working with the PA to build accountable institutions. President Bush was the first U.S. President to call for a two-state solution, and he worked to secure Israeli, Palestinian, and international support and committed the United States to help create the conditions in which two democratic states can live side by side in peace and security.

President Bush urged valued partners like Saudi Arabia to move toward freedom. Saudi Arabia has taken action to confront extremists, along with some initial steps to expand media and religious freedoms. For example, in November 2008, Saudi King Abdallah held a UN meeting on Interfaith Dialogue, in which President Bush participated. Yet Saudi Arabia has a great distance still to travel. The United States will continue to press nations like Saudi Arabia and Egypt to open up their political systems, encourage greater religious tolerance, and give a greater voice to their people.

The President has helped to create international organizations to promote the spread of freedom abroad and more than doubled funding to promote democracy worldwide. The President helped to launch the Asia-Pacific Democracy Partnership (APDP). The APDP will provide a venue in which free nations can work together to support democratic values, strengthen democratic institutions, and assist those who are working to build and sustain free societies across the Asia Pacific region.

President Bush supported the inspiring strides that Europe took toward a continent whole, free, and at peace. Over the past eight years, the United States supported nations from the Baltic to the Black Sea reach their goals of membership in NATO and the European Union. The Administration supported the emergence of democracies in Georgia and Ukraine through its support for civil society and democratic activists during the successful Rose Revolution in Georgia and Orange Revolution in Ukraine and continues to contribute to the strengthening of democracy in both countries. In the wake of Russia's August 2008 invasion of Georgia, President Bush supported Georgia's sovereignty, territorial integrity, and economic recovery, including a $1 billion economic and humanitarian support package. The Administration helped establish Kosovo as an independent, multi-ethnic democracy.

The United States Stood Up For People Suffering Under Oppression

The President met human rights activists from more than 35 countries.

President Bush focused international attention and applied tough sanctions on oppressive regimes in Burma, Belarus, Cuba, Zimbabwe, and other nations and bolstered civil society activists in countries such as China, Cuba, and Venezuela. The United States imposed travel and financial sanctions on repressive regimes, select individuals, and those who provide them with material support. The President established the Commission for Assistance to a Free Cuba to reassure the Cuban people that the United States stands ready to help them transition toward democracy and provided more than $400 million to promote freedom and democracy in Cuba. He also supported pro-democracy forces in Venezuela, Bolivia, and Nicaragua.

The United States is leading the global response to the crisis in Darfur. The United States is the leading international donor to Sudan, providing more than $5 billion in assistance to Sudan since 2005, including $3.7 billion in humanitarian and peacekeeping assistance to Darfur. In 2008, the United States provided half of the World Food Program's food aid request for more than 6 million people throughout Sudan and eastern Chad. In FY 2007, the United States gave more than $1 billion in assistance to the people of Sudan, including Darfur. Since 2004, direct and indirect U.S. support provided to peacekeeping operations in Darfur has totaled more than $600 million.

President Bush announced steps to help the Burmese people bring peaceful change and democratic transition to their country, where a military junta has imposed a 19-year reign of fear. The President and First Lady Laura Bush have been leading advocates for human rights in Burma. The United States has increased its support for Burmese struggling for freedom. The United States has also tightened existing economic sanctions and levied new sanctions against the leaders of the regime and their financial backers; imposed sanctions on state-owned enterprises; imposed an expanded visa ban on those responsible for the most egregious violations of human rights, as well as their family members; called on the Government of Burma to uphold its obligations to the UN Security Council; and facilitated the efforts of humanitarian groups working to alleviate suffering in Burma. Mrs. Bush was also active in supporting the Burmese people's demands for reconciliation and basic human rights such as freedom of speech, worship, association, and assembly. Mrs. Bush hosted an event at the UN headquarters to draw international attention to human rights abuses in Burma.

It is in the best interests of our Nation to alleviate the despair that can allow extremism to take hold by fighting hunger and disease, supporting basic education initiatives, and advancing global economic development. President Bush has more than doubled official development assistance since 2001 and invested more than $6.7 billion in 35 countries around the world that govern justly, invest in their people, and respect economic freedom through the Millennium Challenge Account. President Bush took unprecedented steps to fight disease through the President's Emergency Plan for AIDS Relief, the President's Malaria Initiative, the International Partnership on Avian and Pandemic Influenza, and his initiative to combat neglected tropical diseases. In addition, the United States opened markets for trade and investment to create economic opportunity and lift people out of poverty and has expanded support for basic education initiatives. The President also increased the budget for the National Endowment for Democracy by more than 150 percent since 2001.

Transforming Our Armed Forces
To Face The Threats Of Today And Tomorrow

Over The Past Eight Years, America's Military Has Become Stronger, More Agile, And Better Prepared To Confront Threats To The American People

Following the attacks of 9/11, President Bush strengthened and reshaped our approach to national security. To harden our defense, President Bush:

- Created the Department of Homeland Security;
- Provided national security professionals with vital new tools like the Patriot Act and a program to monitor terrorist communications;
- Reorganized the intelligence community to better meet the needs of the war on terror;
- Deployed aggressive financial measures to freeze terrorist assets; and
- Launched diplomatic initiatives to pressure adversaries and attract new partners to our cause.

➢ **The President made dramatic changes to both our national security strategy and the military itself.** President Bush concluded that we are engaged in an ideological struggle and launched an effort to discredit the hateful vision of the extremists and advance the hopeful alternative of freedom. In order to stay a step ahead of our enemies, the Administration transformed our military both to prevail on the battlefields of today and to meet the threats of tomorrow.

The President Has Transformed Our Military To Become Better Trained, Better Equipped, And Better Prepared For The Threats Of Today, Tomorrow, And Beyond

The United States is arming its troops with the intelligence, weapons, training, and support they need to face a different kind of enemy. The President has equipped our troops with real-time battlefield intelligence capabilities – unimaginable just a few years ago. In Iraq and Afghanistan, troops in the field have used advanced technologies like Global Positioning Systems to direct airstrikes that take out the enemy while sparing the innocent, and the Administration is arming Predator drones and using them to track down terrorists. When President Bush took office, the United States had fewer than 170 unmanned aerial vehicles. Today, that number has expanded to more than 6,000.

➢ **The Administration has expanded the U.S. Special Operations Forces.** President Bush has more than doubled funding for special operations and created the first-ever special operations command within the Marines. Additionally, he has given the Special Operations Command the lead role in the global war on terror.

➢ **Under the President's leadership, the United States has also placed a new focus on counterinsurgency.** General David Petraeus wrote a new counterinsurgency manual published by the Army, with central objectives to gain the support of the people and train local forces to take responsibility on their own. The counterinsurgency strategy also stresses the importance of following security gains with real benefits into the daily lives of citizens.
- The Administration created Provincial Reconstruction Teams (PRTs), which are helping local communities in Iraq and Afghanistan to create jobs, deliver basic services, and prevent terrorists from returning.

➢ **The President has transformed the education and training U.S. troops receive.** Every branch of the military now receives the counterinsurgency training that was once reserved for Special Operations Forces.

Additionally, the President has been transforming the military to confront the challenges ahead. This Administration began the most sweeping transformation of America's global force posture since the end of World War II. Troops are shifting from Cold War garrisons in Europe and Asia, in order to surge more rapidly to troubled spots around the world. President Bush established new military commands to meet challenges unique to Africa and protect the United States. This Administration has also invested more than a half trillion dollars in research and development, to build even more advanced capabilities to protect America. U.S. forces are becoming more joint and interoperable, in order to cooperate seamlessly across different services and with foreign partners. Additionally, the Federal Government is cooperating closely with the private sector to improve security in cyberspace to confront an emerging threat to the U.S. economy, defense systems, and citizens.

➢ **In 2001, President Bush withdrew the United States from the Anti Ballistic Missile Treaty.** As a result, America has developed and deployed new defenses capable of protecting U.S. cities from ballistic missile attack. This system can now defend the United States against limited missile attacks from Northeast Asia. The United States has also concluded agreements with Poland and the Czech Republic to establish missile defense sites on their territories to help protect against ballistic missile attacks from the Middle East.

➢ **The President also worked with Russia to make historic reductions in offensive nuclear weapons.** Following these reductions, the total U.S. nuclear stockpile will be at the lowest level since the Eisenhower Administration. These reductions are part of a new approach to strategic deterrence that relies on both nuclear and conventional strike forces, as well as strong defenses.

Thanks To Our Military, Terrorists Have Suffered Defeats Across The World

Under President Bush, the United States went on the offense against the terrorists overseas, rather than wait for our country to be attacked again. Recognizing the need for strong partners, we helped strengthen the counterterrorism capabilities of our allies and made clear that hostile regimes sponsoring terror or pursuing weapons of mass destruction would be held to account. The United States and its allies have applied the full range of our military and intelligence assets to keep pressure on al Qaeda and its affiliates. They have:
- Severely weakened the terrorists;
- Disrupted plots to attack our homeland; and
- Captured or killed hundreds of al Qaeda leaders and operatives in more than two dozen countries, including Khalid Sheikh Mohammed, the mastermind of the 9/11 attacks.

The United States has helped key partners and allies strengthen their capabilities in the fight against the terrorists. Intelligence sharing has increased with friends and allies around the world, and training and support has been provided to counterterrorism partners who have made substantial contributions to the war on terror, such as the Philippines, Indonesia, Jordan, and Saudi Arabia.

President Bush has made clear that governments that sponsor terror are as guilty as the terrorists and will be held to account. Following 9/11, the President applied this doctrine to Afghanistan and removed the Taliban from power, shut down al Qaeda training camps, and liberated more than 25 million Afghans. Today, the United States, its 25 NATO allies, and 17 partner nations are standing with the Afghan people as they defend their free society.

➢ **In Iraq, the United States acted with a coalition of nations to protect the American people and liberated more than 25 million Iraqis.** Just last week, Iraq approved two agreements that formalize diplomatic, economic, and security ties with America, and set a framework for the drawdown of American forces as the fight in Iraq nears a successful end.

Recognizing that the only way to defeat the terrorists in the long run is to present an alternative to their hateful ideology, the United States is helping democratic societies emerge as examples for people across the Middle East. President Bush is pressing nations around the world – including our friends – to allow their citizens to have greater freedom of speech, worship, and assembly. Additionally, the Administration is advancing a broader vision of reform that includes economic prosperity, quality health care and education, vibrant civil societies, and women's rights.

The Bush Administration Has
Provided Unprecedented Support For Our Veterans

"One of the things I have treasured the most is to be the Commander-in-Chief of men and women of courage and character and decency." **President George W. Bush (December 6, 2008)**

President Bush has remained committed to ensuring all veterans receive the care and support they need from the Federal government. Under his leadership, the Administration has:

Dramatically Increased Funding To Support And Care For Those Who Have Served Our Nation
- Increased funding for veterans' medical care by more than 115 percent since 2001.
- FY 2009 funding for the Department of Veterans Affairs (VA) totals more than $97 billion, nearly double the level of funding when the President took office and the highest level of support for veterans in history.
- Provided more than $6 billion to modernize and expand VA medical facilities and more than $1 billion over the past three years to support traumatic brain injury and post-traumatic stress disorder treatment and research.
- Honored our veterans with a hallowed, final resting place by implementing and fully funding the largest expansion in the national cemetery system since the Civil War.

Improved Care And Services For Wounded Warriors
- Created the Commission on Care for America's Returning Wounded Warriors – co-chaired by former Senator Bob Dole and former Health and Human Services Secretary Donna Shalala – to ensure that wounded service members and veterans receive quality care and services and can live lives of hope, promise, and dignity. Nearly all of the Commission's recommendations have already been implemented, such as:
    - Expanded training, screening, and staff resources to help service members and veterans suffering from mental health disorders.
    - Created a joint Recovery Coordinator Program for seriously injured service members.
    - Initiated a pilot program to replace the cumbersome system of two separate disability examinations with a single, comprehensive medical exam.
- Established a Center of Excellence for Psychological Health and Traumatic Brain Injury and expanded VA's polytrauma system of care to 21 network sites and clinic support teams to provide state-of-the-art treatment to injured veterans at facilities closer to their homes.

Ensured Those Who Have Served Our Country Receive The Benefits They Deserve
- Called for and signed a GI Bill for the 21st century, which expanded education benefits for service members and veterans and made it easier for those who defend our Nation to transfer unused education benefits to their spouses or children.
- Increased career counseling services for returning veterans, particularly those wounded in combat.
- Signed legislation that increased from two to five years a combat veteran's eligibility to enroll for lifetime VA medical care and allowed family members of injured service members to take additional time away from their jobs to care for their loved ones.
- Signed legislation to ensure military retirees with severe disabilities receive both their military retired pay and their VA disability compensation.
- Helped more than 1.9 million veterans enroll in the VA health care system since 2001.
- Reduced the average length of time to process a veteran's disability claim to under 180 days, down from 230 days when the President took office.

Worked To Decrease The Number Of Homeless Veterans
- Expanded Federal grants and worked extensively with faith-based and community organizations to help homeless veterans.
- Cut the number of homeless veterans by nearly 40 percent from 2001 to 2007.

Defending Against Weapons Of Mass Destruction Terrorism

➢ **After September 11, 2001, the President recognized the need to change our strategy to address the new challenges of terrorism and proliferation.** In 2002, the President put forth a comprehensive strategy to combat WMD, and in 2006, he established objectives tailored to meet the threat of WMD Terrorism (WMD-T):

- Determine terrorists' intentions, capabilities, and plans to acquire and develop WMD.
- Deny terrorists access to the materials, expertise, and other enabling capabilities needed to develop WMD.
- Deter terrorists from employing WMD.
- Detect and disrupt terrorists' attempted movement of WMD-related materials, weapons, and personnel.
- Prevent and be prepared to respond to WMD-related terrorist attacks.
- Develop the capability to determine the nature and scope of a terrorist-employed device.

➢ **To effectuate this strategy, the Administration launched numerous initiatives including:**

- The Proliferation Security Initiative;
- The Global Initiative for Combating Nuclear Terrorism;
- Threat reduction programs with countries in the former Soviet Union; and
- Intelligence community reforms.

The United States Has Made Significant Progress in Implementing Each Pillar Of This Strategy

➢ **The Administration has reorganized and integrated the Intelligence Community under the Director of National Intelligence to provide a clearer picture of terrorist capabilities and intentions, including with respect to WMD.** The Administration established the National Counterterrorism Center (NCTC), and it also created a National Counterproliferation Center (NCPC) to cover the entire range of proliferation challenges. At the State Department, the WMD-T office was created to help partner nations assess risks from WMD and work with foreign governments to ensure continuous improvement in our collective capabilities to reduce risks from WMD-T.

➢ **The Administration is denying access to the materials and capabilities required to develop WMD through unparalleled international outreach and cooperation.** The President has created strong international partnerships such as the 2005 Bratislava Initiative, which accelerated and expanded bilateral nuclear security cooperation in five areas: emergency response, best practices, security culture, conversion of Russian-origin research reactors in third countries, and Russian nuclear security. In addition:

- o The Administration provided assistance to Russia and other states of the former Soviet Union to improve security and accounting of nuclear weapons and materials. In addition, U.S. and Russian nuclear stockpiles have been reduced.
- o The Administration has created international partnerships and helped convert 51 nuclear reactors in 29 countries from highly enriched uranium to low-enriched uranium, which cannot be used to produce nuclear weapons. The United States has also secured more than 600 vulnerable sites around the world that together contain enough material to make about 8,000 radiological, or "dirty" bombs.
- o In 2004, the Global Threat Reduction Initiative (GTRI) was developed, accelerating efforts to identify, secure, and remove high-risk vulnerable nuclear and radiological materials around the world. We have redirected former Soviet biological weapons scientists to peaceful, sustainable employment and reconfigured former facilities to accelerate drug and vaccine development for infectious diseases.
- o In 2006, the United States and Russia launched the Global Initiative to Combat Nuclear Terrorism, which is helping to build international capacity to prevent, defend against, and respond to nuclear terrorism. Today, 75 nations are working under this initiative.
- o The Administration has been at the forefront of efforts to enhance the effectiveness of the Biological Weapons Convention (BWC). The United States has developed an active, "real-world" work plan and developed model legislation on BWC prohibitions and pathogen security.

➤ **The United States is working to detect and to disrupt terrorists' attempted movement of WMD-related materials, weapons, and personnel through innovative initiatives.** Under the President's leadership, the United States launched:
  o The Proliferation Security Initiative to stem the flow of illicit materials used for weapons of mass destruction and their delivery systems. More than 90 nations are now partners in this effort.
  o The Container Security Initiative (CSI) to detect the movement of dangerous materials in foreign countries and stop them before they are placed on vessels destined for the United States.
  o The Megaports Initiative to provide key ports around the world with radiation detection equipment.
  o The Domestic Nuclear Detection Office (DNDO) to improve the Nation's capability to detect and report nuclear or radiological material intended for use against the Nation. As part of a layered defense strategy, the Administration also effectively doubled the national response capacity to disable improvised WMD.
  o The Nuclear Materials Information Program to provide an enduring, centralized, and properly vetted source of information on nuclear materials worldwide.

➤ **The Administration is employing an effective deterrence strategy tailored to the WMD-T threat by putting the terrorists, their facilitators, and their sponsors on notice of the United States' response in the event of an attack, to include holding any state, group, or non-state actors fully accountable for supporting or enabling terrorist efforts to obtain or use WMD.** The Administration has also established a national technical nuclear forensics center within the DNDO and the National Bioforensics Center within the National Biodefense Analysis and Countermeasures Center in the Department of Homeland Security (DHS) in order to facilitate forensic investigation and attribution of WMD-related materials.

➤ **The Administration has recognized the need to build our prevention and response capabilities in the event of a WMD-related terrorist attack.** Through new technologies, assistance to State and local health professionals, and an unprecedented Federal funding commitment, the Administration launched the following:
  o The Department of Homeland Security, Environmental Protection Agency, and the Department of Health and Human Services (HHS) deployed the first ever bioaerosol monitoring system – Biowatch – to more than 30 major metropolitan areas to provide early warning of an attack and enable quick response.
  o HHS created a laboratory response network of approximately 170 public health laboratories nationwide to assist in detecting disease outbreaks that could be associated with bioterrorism attacks.
  o The Defense Secretary has certified 53 National Guard WMD civil support teams stationed across the United States, including the District of Columbia and the U.S. territories.
  o President Bush has expanded funding for anti-bioterrorism research at the National Institutes for Health from $53 million in 2001 to more than $1.7 billion annually to study threat agents and other novel or emerging pathogens.
  o Project Bioshield was launched in 2004 with $5.6 billion in funding over 10 years for the acquisition of medical countermeasures, and in 2006, the Biomedical Advanced Research and Development Authority was created to manage the development and acquisition of needed vaccines, drugs, and diagnostic tools.
  o The President revitalized the Strategic National Stockpile, increasing funding more than ten-fold since taking office, from $51 million in 2001 to more than $550 million annually, a total investment of more than $3.5 billion.
  o The Administration has stockpiled enough smallpox vaccine for every American and more than 60 million 60-day courses of preventive antibiotics and 5.6 million vaccines regimens against anthrax.
  o HHS has provided $5.2 billion in grants to improve State, local, and tribal health preparedness and mass casualty response capabilities and $3.1 billion in grants to increase hospital preparedness.

➤ **The Administration has led international efforts to detect, prevent, and mitigate the threat of biological terrorism.** Working with at-risk countries, the United States has improved global capabilities to detect, diagnose, and report bioterror attacks and potential pandemics and consolidate and secure their dangerous pathogen collections into safe national-level facilities. The United States has also worked to improve biosafety and biosecurity worldwide;

eliminate biological weapons infrastructure; and focus strategic partnership research to identify and map extremely dangerous indigenous pathogens. In addition, President Bush and his Administration:

- o Expanded efforts to assist countries in the Middle East, South Asia, and Southeast Asia that face significant risks from transnational terrorist groups, have poorly secured biological laboratories and culture collections, and experience frequent outbreaks of emerging infectious diseases.
- o Promoted improved diagnostics and biosurveillance in key regions; enhanced U.S. response and host nation capabilities to respond to a biological incident overseas; and trained foreign partners in forensic epidemiology as a key to respond to bioterrorism incidents globally.
- o Eliminated bio-weapons-related infrastructure and equipment in Stepnogorsk, Kazakhstan; Tabakhmela, Georgia; and Vozrozhdeniye Island, Uzbekistan; consolidated dangerous pathogen collections and research in Azerbaijan, Georgia, and Uzbekistan, with efforts underway in Kazakhstan and Ukraine. We have also transferred dangerous pathogens from Georgia, Azerbaijan, Kazakhstan, and Uzbekistan to U.S. biodefense research laboratories.

- ➢ **Since 2001, the President has continued to strengthen domestic lab security.** The Administration has instituted laboratory safety and security guidelines to manage the risks posed by accidental infection of researchers, intentional theft, or diversion of materials that could enable a catastrophic bioterrorism attack.
  - o HHS and the Department of Agriculture have identified those select agents and toxins that present significant bioterrorism risk and increased security requirements accordingly.
  - o The Administration created the National Science Advisory Board for Biosecurity (NSABB) to advise the U.S. government on strategies for minimizing the potential for misuse of information and technologies from life sciences research, taking into consideration both national security concerns and the needs of the research community. The NSABB currently is developing recommendations to enhance personnel reliability practices at domestic institutes that store or work with select agents and toxins.
  - o Since the inception of the Select Agent Program in 2002, the Centers for Disease Control and Animal and Plant Health Inspection Service (APHIS) have executed inspections and re-inspections for all of the approximately 400 registered entities in the United States working with designated Select Agents pathogens and toxins.

While Significant Progress Has Been Made, Challenges Remain

America must continue to build upon this progress and remain vigilant in our efforts to meet this dynamic threat.
- o The United States must accelerate the implementation of ODNI and NCTC initiatives to refine our intelligence on nuclear and biological WMD terrorism threats, trends, and related issues.
- o The United States also must take steps to reinvigorate our aging nuclear expertise and supporting infrastructure to ensure we have an enduring capability to support nuclear intelligence, technical forensics, and attribution activities.
- o Through U.S. leadership, we must maintain the world's focus and attention to ensure that WMD and the means to deliver them do not reach the hands of the world's most dangerous enemies.

President Bush's Global Health Initiatives Are Saving Lives Around The World

President Bush Helped Save Millions Of Lives Through The President's Emergency Plan For AIDS Relief And The President's Malaria Initiative

America Has Led An Unprecedented Effort To Combat HIV/AIDS Around The World

President Bush has made a historic commitment to the fight against global HIV/AIDS. In his 2003 State of the Union Address, President Bush announced the President's Emergency Plan for AIDS Relief (PEPFAR) to combat global HIV/AIDS. Later that year, President Bush signed the initial 5-year, $15 billion authorizing legislation that had been approved with strong bipartisan support. This President views this commitment as a central part of our foreign policy to help alleviate the despair that allows extremism to take hold.

PEPFAR is the largest international health initiative in history to fight a single disease. This effort has helped bring life-saving treatment to more than 2.1 million people and care for more than 10 million people – including more than four million orphans and vulnerable children – around the world. PEPFAR's success is rooted in U.S. support for local programs that use the power of partnerships among governments, foundations, non-governmental organizations, faith-based groups, and the private sector.

➢ **As of September 30, 2008, PEPFAR was supporting life-saving antiretroviral treatment for more than two million people living with HIV/AIDS in Sub-Saharan Africa.** When the President announced PEPFAR in 2003, only 50,000 people in all of Sub-Saharan Africa were receiving antiretroviral treatment.

➢ **Through Fiscal Year 2008, PEPFAR has also:**
  - Supported prevention of mother-to-child HIV transmission for women during more than 16 million pregnancies.
  - Supported prevention of nearly 240,000 infant infections.
  - Supported more than 57 million counseling and testing sessions for men, women, and children.

➢ **PEPFAR draws upon the capabilities of faith- and community-based organizations to create an effective, multi-sectoral response to the HIV/AIDS pandemic.** These organizations are uniquely positioned to promote HIV/AIDS stigma reduction and prevention messages and provide counseling and testing, home care, clinical services, and antiretroviral treatment with particular success in the hardest-to-reach communities. Last year, 87 percent of PEPFAR partners were indigenous organizations, and nearly a quarter were faith-based.

➢ **PEPFAR supports a comprehensive prevention portfolio.** In addition to the balanced, evidenced-based ABC (Abstain, Be faithful, and correct and consistent use of Condoms) approach, the United States also supports programs that address mother-to-child transmission, blood safety and safe medical injections, male circumcision, injecting drug users, HIV-discordant couples, alcohol abuse, and other key issues.

On July 30, 2008, President Bush signed legislation to reauthorize PEPFAR, authorizing an additional $48 billion over the next five years to combat global HIV/AIDS, tuberculosis, and malaria. Under this legislation, the next phase of the American people's generous commitment to those suffering from HIV/AIDS will support:
  - Treatment for at least three million people;
  - Prevention of 12 million new infections; and
  - Care for 12 million people, including five million orphans and vulnerable children.

As a result of the President's leadership, in 2007, G-8 leaders made a commitment to complement U.S. efforts so that together G-8 nations will support treatment for five million HIV/AIDS-infected individuals, prevent 24 million new infections, and care for 24 million people, including 10 million orphans and vulnerable children.

The United States is also working through multilateral organizations in the global fight against HIV/AIDS. The United States is the largest contributor to the Global Fund for HIV/AIDS, Malaria, and Tuberculosis, pledging $4 billion and providing more than $3.3 billion since 2001.

The Administration And Its Partners Have Worked Together To Save Lives Through The President's Malaria Initiative

In 2005, President Bush launched the President's Malaria Initiative (PMI), committing $1.2 billion over five years to reduce malaria deaths by 50 percent in 15 targeted African countries. The President has also challenged the private sector to join the fight against malaria. It is estimated that the PMI has already reached 25 million people in Sub-Saharan Africa.

In 2007, more than six million long-lasting, insecticide-treated mosquito nets were distributed through public-private partnerships to which PMI contributed.

The United States is leading the way in the efforts against malaria and has urged other nations to join. In 2007, G-8 nations matched the United States' commitment so that together, G-8 nations will work to cut malaria deaths in 30 countries by half. As part of fulfilling these and other commitments on malaria, in 2008, G-8 nations agreed to provide 100 million bed nets by the end of 2010 in partnership with other stakeholders. G-8 nations should continue to take action on these promises.

In 2006, President and Mrs. Bush hosted a White House Summit on Malaria to discuss and highlight measures for combating this preventable disease. This summit brought together international experts, multilateral institutions, corporations and foundations, African civic leaders, NGOs, and faith-based and service organizations to discuss and highlight measures for controlling malaria.

President Bush's Initiatives Are Providing More Effective Resources For Health Around The World

In 2008, President Bush announced a new initiative to combat neglected tropical diseases (NTDs) around the world. This Initiative committed $350 million available over five years to provide integrated treatment for more than 300 million people in Africa, Asia, and Latin America, targeting seven major NTDs: lymphatic filariasis (elephantiasis); schistosomiasis (snail fever); trachoma (eye infection); onchocerciasis (river blindness); and three soil-transmitted helminthes (STHs – hookworm, roundworm, whipworm).

President Bush successfully challenged other nations to join the NTD effort. At their summit on June 10, 2008, the United States and the European Union announced that they would join together to combat NTDs. In July 2008, G-8 leaders committed to join the United States in fighting NTDs by working to support the control or elimination of NTDs in order to reach at least 75 percent of people affected with certain major NTDs in Africa, Asia, and Latin America. In September 2008, the United Kingdom announced a £50 million commitment to NTDs, citing the contribution built upon President Bush's $350 million announcement and his call to the G-8.

In 2008, President Bush and U.K. Prime Minister Gordon Brown announced a commitment to work together alongside other partners to fight diseases and support stronger health systems, public and private sector health institutions, and health workers. The United States and European Union announced on June 10 that they would work together to support partner countries to strengthen health systems and improve availability of appropriately trained health workers.

President Bush worked with international partners such as Australia, Canada, the European Union, and Japan to ensure a coordinated response to a potential outbreak of avian or pandemic flu.

As part of his "Advancing the Cause of Social Justice in the Western Hemisphere," President Bush launched new healthcare initiatives for Latin America, including ordering the USNS Comfort to Latin America and the Caribbean on a Humanitarian Mission in 2007. Alongside the USNS Comfort medical crew were staff from the Department of Health and Human Services and volunteers from U.S. non-governmental organizations such as Project Hope and Operation Smile to provide free health care services to communities in need over a four-month deployment to the region. More than 98,000 people received care during this deployment. In 2007, the United States also opened the first regional healthcare training center in Panama. This innovative U.S. health diplomacy program trains nurses, technicians, and community health workers from six Central American countries.

President Bush Helped Americans Through Tax Relief

President Bush Trusted Americans With Their Hard-Earned Money, Providing $1.7 Trillion In Relief Through 2008

President Bush demonstrated that letting people keep more of their own money leads to economic growth. In 2001, America was experiencing the unprecedented triple shock of a recession following the dot-com bust, economic disruption due to the terrorist attacks of September 11, and corporate accounting scandals. Fortunately, the country was able to overcome these challenges, in part because President Bush's tax relief put more money in families' pockets and encouraged businesses to grow and invest. Following the President's 2003 tax relief, the United States had 52 months of uninterrupted job growth, the longest run on record.

President Bush Signed The Largest Tax Relief In A Generation

President Bush's tax cuts provided $1.7 trillion in relief through 2008. President Bush worked with Congress to reduce the tax burden on American families and small businesses to spur savings, investment, and job creation.

In 2001, President Bush proposed and signed the Economic Growth and Tax Relief Reconciliation Act. This legislation:
- Reduced tax rates for every American who pays income taxes, including creating a new 10 percent tax bracket
- Doubled the child tax credit to $1,000 by 2010
- Reduced the marriage penalty beginning in 2005
- Put the death tax on the road to extinction
- Increased education tax benefits
- Increased limits on IRA and 401(k) contributions and changed limits on defined benefit pension plans – which were made permanent in the Pension Protection Act of 2006

In 2003, President Bush proposed and signed the Jobs and Growth Tax Relief Reconciliation Act. This legislation:
- Reduced the top tax rate on dividends and capital gains to 15 percent
- Accelerated income tax rate reductions
- Accelerated the expansion of the 10 percent bracket
- Accelerated the increase of the child credit to $1,000
- Accelerated the reduction in the marriage penalty
- Quadrupled small business expensing from $25,000 to $100,000
- Increased bonus depreciation for businesses to 50 percent through 2004

President Bush's Tax Relief Allowed Americans To Keep Trillions Of Dollars Of Their Own Money

Results of the President's tax relief were swift. The economy returned to growth in the fourth quarter of 2001 and continued to grow for 24 consecutive quarters. The economy grew at a rapid pace of 7.5 percent above inflation during the third quarter of 2003 – the highest since 1984. The President's tax relief reduced the marginal effective tax rate on new investment, which encourages additional investment and, in the long-term, higher wages for workers.

➢ **In 2007, a family of four earning $40,000 saved an average of $2,053 thanks to the President's tax relief.**

The President's tax relief was followed by increases in tax revenue. From 2005 to 2007, tax revenues grew faster than the economy. The ratio of receipts to GDP rose to 18.8 percent in 2007, above the 40-year average. Between 2004 and 2006, capital gains realizations grew by approximately 60 percent. Growth in corporate income tax receipts was especially strong in the President's second term, nearly doubling between 2004 and 2007 and contributing a full percentage point to the increase in the total federal receipts-to-GDP share.

The President's tax relief has shifted a larger share of the individual income taxes paid to higher-income taxpayers. With nearly all of the tax relief provisions fully in effect, the President's tax relief reduced the share of taxes paid by the bottom 50 percent of taxpayers from 3.9 percent in 2000 to 3.1 percent in 2005, the latest year of available data, while increasing the share paid by the top 10 percent from 46.0 to 46.4 percent.

President Bush Led The Response To The Financial Crisis Of 2008

This unprecedented economic growth was ended by the turbulence in the housing and credit markets, to which the President responded with bold action. President Bush addressed the weakness in the economy early in 2008 by leading the bipartisan passage of an economic growth package that boosted consumer spending and encouraged businesses to expand, returning more than $96 billion to Americans. When the financial crisis intensified, President Bush led the passage and implementation of a rescue plan that helped address the root of the financial crisis, protected the deposits of individuals and small businesses, and helped enable credit to remain available to individuals and families. Moreover, he convened a summit with the leaders of the G-20 nations to discuss efforts to strengthen economic growth, deal with the financial crisis, reaffirm a commitment to free market principles, and lay the foundation for reform to help ensure that a similar crisis does not happen again.

➢ **The Administration warned of the risk that government-sponsored enterprises (GSEs) Fannie Mae and Freddie Mac posed to America's financial security beginning in 2001.** President Bush's first budget warned that "financial trouble of a large GSE could cause strong repercussions in financial markets." In 2003, the Administration began calling for a new GSE regulator. Despite resistance from Congress, President Bush continued to call for GSE reform until Congress finally acted in 2008 to provide the additional oversight the President requested five years earlier. Unfortunately, the reform came too late to prevent systemic consequences.

President Bush Expanded And Enforced Trade Agreements To Open New Markets For American Products

The President Has Enacted New Free Trade Agreements That Are Benefitting American Farmers, Workers, And Small Business Owners

The President leveled the playing field for American workers by increasing the number of countries partnered with the U.S. on free trade agreements (FTAs) from three to 16. One additional agreement has been approved by Congress but is not yet in force and agreements with three countries are awaiting Congressional approval. Thanks in part to President Bush's leadership on free trade, America's exports now account for a larger percentage of our Gross Domestic Product than at any other time on record.

The United States currently has trade agreements in force with:
- Israel
- Canada
- Mexico
- Jordan
- Chile
- Singapore
- Australia
- Morocco
- El Salvador
- Guatemala
- Honduras
- Nicaragua
- Dominican Republic
- Bahrain
- Oman
- Costa Rica

Overall goods and services exports have increased by more than 50 percent between 2000 and 2007 to a level that accounts for more than 13 percent of our GDP, greater than any time in history. Exports to the 11 trade partners with FTAs that went into effect between 2001 and 2007 grew more than 70 percent faster on average than U.S. exports to the rest of the world during the periods in which the FTAs were in effect. President Bush opened new markets for American farmers and ranchers, which helped create a record level of U.S. agricultural exports of $92.4 billion in 2007, up more than 70 percent since 2000. In addition, he ensured other countries abided by trade rules and won or settled 24 trade disputes brought by the United States to the World Trade Organization since 2001.

This Administration negotiated and signed a trade agreement that helped increase U.S. exports to Central America by nearly $8 billion from 2005 to 2008. U.S. exports to Central America dramatically increased following initial entry into force of the Dominican Republic-Central America-United States Free Trade Agreement (CAFTA-DR). CAFTA countries increased their annual goods exports to the U.S. from $14.7 billion in 2005 to an annualized $15.6 billion in 2008, an increase of 6.5 percent, which has supported jobs in the region.

No Child Left Behind Has Raised Expectations And Improved Results

Since No Child Left Behind Took Effect, Test Scores Have Risen, Accountability Has Increased, And The Achievement Gap Between White And Minority Students Has Narrowed

In 2002, President Bush signed the bipartisan No Child Left Behind Act (NCLB). This groundbreaking, bipartisan law brought Republicans and Democrats together to expand opportunities for American children of all backgrounds and provide all our children with the quality education they deserve while preserving local control. President Bush transformed the Federal government's approach to education through No Child Left Behind. The results are clear: African American and Hispanic students have posted all-time highs in a number of categories.

➤ **President Bush believes we must have high expectations for every student.** He has provided increased Federal education funding to schools so they can help our students reach these expectations. He has given parents more information about schools and more say in how their children are educated. As a result, under NCLB, all students have a better chance to learn, excel, and achieve their dreams.

➤ *No Child Left Behind* **has increased accountability by requiring all schools to help all of their students meet State-set standards.** It has focused our national conversation on education on results. When President Bush took office in 2001, only 11 States were in full compliance with the previous Federal accountability requirements, and some did not even participate in the Nation's Report Card or the National Assessment of Educational Progress. Little objective data was available to know whether our students were acquiring at least grade-level skills. Today:
  - All 50 States, the District of Columbia, and Puerto Rico have accountability plans in place;
  - All 50 States, D.C., and Puerto Rico assess public school students annually in grades 3-8 and once in high school to measure progress toward grade-level proficiency;
  - All 50 States, D.C., and Puerto Rico offer parents "report cards" on their public schools; and
  - All 50 States, D.C., and Puerto Rico participate in the Nation's Report Card.

NCLB Has Worked For Children Of All Backgrounds, In Every Part Of The Country

As the 2007 Nation's Report Card shows, NCLB is helping raise achievement for all kinds of children, in all kinds of schools. Minority students, low-income students, and students with disabilities have shown improvements in a number of areas. As a result, the achievement gap is narrowing.

➤ **President Bush confronted the soft bigotry of low expectations.** The Nation's Report Card shows African-American students, Hispanic students, and students with disabilities are progressing in many categories.
  - In fourth-grade reading, the achievement gap between white and African-American students is at an all-time low.
  - In math, fourth- and eighth-grade African-American students achieved their highest scores to date.
  - In fourth-grade reading and in fourth and eighth-grade math, Hispanic students set new achievement records. In reading, Hispanic eighth-graders matched their all-time high.
  - Average reading scores for fourth-grade students with disabilities improved 23 points between 2000 and 2007.

➤ **Through NCLB, we have invested more in our schools, and we are expecting and getting results nationwide.** The Nation's Report Card shows improvement in fourth- and eighth-grade reading and math achievement.
  - Since 2002, fourth-graders have shown significant increases in reading achievement, with the highest rate of improvement coming among lower-performing students. As a result, in 2007, U.S. fourth-graders achieved their highest reading scores on record.
  - All students are increasing achievement in math. Since 2003, significant gains in math have occurred for both higher- and lower-performing children in both fourth- and eighth grades, and in 2007, both fourth- and eighth-graders posted their highest math scores on record.
  - Nearly one million more students have learned basic math skills since the law was passed.

NCLB Put America's Schools On A New Path Of Reform And A New Path to Results, Via Four Key Principles:

➢ **Every child can learn, we expect every child to learn, and we must hold ourselves accountable for every child's education.** We must assess whether a child can read and do math at grade level. Under NCLB, when we find that students in a particular school are not learning, we give that school time, incentives, and resources to improve. The school must do whatever is necessary to help students reach grade level by 2014.
  - Support for Title I Grants to high-poverty schools is stronger than ever at $14.3 billion, an increase of 63 percent since the enactment of NCLB.
  - Support for special education programs is $12 billion, an increase of 67 percent since 2001.

➢ **Government must trust parents to make the right decisions for their children.** For reform to be meaningful, parents must have real options to choose the best schools to meet their child's individual needs. Under NCLB, if a school does not perform or improve, a parent has the option to choose a better public school, a public charter school, or a tutor. To ensure these options are available and of high quality, President Bush has provided more than $1.6 billion to help support charter schools, which has helped contribute to the number of charter schools nationwide more than doubling since 2000. The President also established the D.C. Opportunity Scholarships program, the first Federal school-choice program, which has provided more than 2,600 students with scholarships to attend the private or religious school of their choice.

➢ **NCLB established the principle that Federal funding should be invested in programs that have rigorous research demonstrating their effectiveness.** Reading First has provided more than $6 billion to fund scientifically-based instructional programs, valid and reliable diagnostic assessments, and professional development for teachers. State data shows that Reading First students from nearly every grade and subgroup have made impressive gains in reading proficiency. For first grade, 44 of 50 States reported increases in the percentage of students proficient in reading comprehension; for second grade, 39 of 52 States reported improvement; and for third grade, 27 of 35 States reported improvement.

➢ **The Federal government must trust local educators and provide flexibility to States and school districts.** Under NCLB, States must set high standards and hold schools accountable for results, and the Federal government supports both these activities with increased resources and flexibility. Over the past several years, the Administration has created a series of new pilot programs and regulations that further increase this flexibility, such as the Growth Model Pilot, which allows schools to get credit for individual student progress.

Strengthening NCLB For The Future

In 2007, the President released *Building on Results: A Blueprint for Strengthening the No Child Left Behind Act*, which proposed common-sense improvements to NCLB. The President's plan called on Congress to:
  - Strengthen efforts to close the achievement gap through high standards, accountability, and more information for parents.
  - Give States flexibility to better measure individual student progress, target resources to students most in need, and improve assessments for students with disabilities and limited English proficiency.
  - Prepare high school students for success in postsecondary education and the 21st century workforce by promoting rigorous and advanced coursework and providing new resources for schools serving low-income students.
  - Provide greater resources for teachers to further close the achievement gap through improved math and science instruction, intensive aid for struggling students, and rewards for exceptional teachers who raise student achievement.
  - Offer additional tools to help local educators turn around chronically underperforming schools and empower parents with better information and increased school choice options.

When Congress failed to reauthorize NCLB, President Bush asked Secretary of Education Margaret Spellings to take a series of administrative steps that would strengthen NCLB and ensure continued progress toward the goal of every child reading and doing math at grade level by 2014.

➢ **The Secretary gave States flexibility to help turn around schools in need of improvement.** In March 2008, the Secretary announced the Differentiated Accountability Pilot, which allows States to differentiate their school interventions based on the academic reasons that have caused schools to be identified as needing improvement.

➢ **New regulations strengthened No Child Left Behind.** Secretary Spellings proposed a package of regulations that address the dropout crisis in America, strengthen accountability, improve our lowest-performing schools, and ensure that more students get access to high-quality tutoring. The regulations, which became final in October 2008, seek to:

- **Address the dropout crisis and ensure accurate reporting of graduation rates.** The regulations build on the work of the National Governor's Association to establish a uniform measure that shows how many incoming freshman in a given high school graduate within four years. All States will use the same formula to calculate how many students graduate from high school on time and how many drop out.

- **Strengthen accountability.** The regulations outline the criteria that States must meet in order to incorporate individual student progress into the State's definition of Adequate Yearly Progress (AYP) and require States and districts to report reading and math results from the most recent National Assessment of Educational Progress to help parents evaluate the performance of their State and district.

- **Improve our lowest-performing schools.** A recent study found that 40 percent of schools in restructuring did not implement any of the restructuring options under the law. The proposed regulations will clarify that restructuring interventions must be more rigorous and that interventions must address the reasons for the restructuring.

- **Increase student access to high-quality tutoring and school choice.** The regulations ensure parents are notified in a clear and timely way about their public school choice and Supplemental Education Service options. The proposed regulations ensure that States and districts make more information available to the public about what tutoring providers are available, how these providers are approved and monitored, and how effective they are in helping students improve.

President Bush Strengthened America's Health Care System

President Bush enacted policies to help Americans receive the care they need at a price they can afford and also infused transparency and innovation into the health care system. The President instituted the most significant reforms to Medicare in nearly 40 years, most notably through a prescription drug benefit, which has provided more than 40 million Americans with better access to prescription drugs. The President also created tax-free Health Savings Accounts to help Americans take charge of their health care decision-making, and increased funding for medical research, which contributed to medical breakthroughs such as the development of the HPV cancer vaccine.

President Bush Reformed Medicare And Added A Prescription Drug Benefit

The President provided more than 40 million Americans with better access to prescription drugs through the market-based Medicare Prescription Drug Benefit. President Bush established competition among private drug plans, which contributed to a 40 percent decline in the actual average 2008 premiums for Medicare drug coverage compared to original estimates. Projected overall program spending between 2004 and 2013 is approximately $240 billion lower, nearly 38 percent, than originally estimated. Furthermore, the President:

- Improved the quality of health care for Medicare beneficiaries by adding preventive screening programs to help diagnose illnesses earlier.
- Increased competition and choices by stabilizing and expanding private plan options through the Medicare Advantage program, and increased enrollment to nearly 10 million Americans. Increased private plan enrollment from 4.7 million in 2003 to nearly 10 million in 2008 (more than 20 percent of all Medicare beneficiaries). The Administration also ensured nearly every county in America has a private plan choice, many with zero dollar premiums and supplemental benefits.

President Bush Pursued Innovative Ways To Make Sure Our Health Care System Meets The Needs Of All Americans

The Administration developed policies that improved the Nation's health care system by making it more affordable, transparent, portable, and efficient. The President:

- Empowered Americans to take charge of their health care decision-making by establishing tax-free Health Savings Accounts (HSAs). This enabled more than six million Americans who have enrolled in HSA-eligible plans to save money tax-free for current and future medical expenses.
- Infused transparency about price and quality into the health care system and launched an initiative to make electronic health records available to most Americans within 10 years. The President also directed Federal agencies to inform beneficiaries of the prices paid to doctors and hospitals and empowered Americans to find better value and better care, largely through increased competition, and he ordered Federal agencies to use improved health IT systems to facilitate the rapid exchange of electronic health information to improve the quality of care for Americans.
- Helped provide treatment to nearly 17 million people by establishing or expanding more than 1,200 community health centers focused in high-poverty areas. Increased the number of patients treated at health centers by more than 60 percent, to nearly 17 million people, since 2001.
- Increased funding at the National Institutes of Health (NIH), the primary Federal agency for medical research, by more than 44 percent since 2001, and fulfilled the commitment to double the NIH budget over the five year period from 1998 to 2003. This contributed to breakthroughs such as the development of the HPV cancer vaccine, advances in cell reprogramming, the development of the Cancer Genome Atlas, and the completion of the Human Genome Project.
- Expanded the Trade Adjustment Assistance program add a tax credit to help displaced workers afford health insurance.

President Bush Provided Unprecedented Resources For Veterans

The President transformed the veterans health care system to better serve those who have sacrificed for our freedom. He instituted reforms for the care of wounded warriors, many of which were based on the recommendations of the Dole-Shalala Commission, and dramatically expanded resources for mental health services. The President:

- Increased funding for veterans' medical care by more than 115 percent since 2001 and committed more than $6 billion to modernize and expand VA medical facilities, ensuring more veterans could receive quality care close to home.
- Created a joint Department of Defense/VA Recovery Coordinator Program for seriously-injured service members.
- Initiated a pilot program to replace the cumbersome system of two separate disability examinations with a single, comprehensive medical exam.
- Expanded training, screening, and staff resources to help service members and veterans suffering from mental health disorders.
- Provided more than $1 billion to VA since 2007 to support traumatic brain injury and post-traumatic stress disorder treatment and research.
- Created the Defense Centers of Excellence for Psychological Health and Traumatic Brain Injury and expanded VA's polytrauma system of care to 22 network sites and clinic support teams to provide state-of-the-art treatment to injured veterans at facilities closer to their homes.
- Expanded VA's use of electronic health records to improve the quality of medical care for veterans.

Empowering Medicare Beneficiaries With Affordable Options

President Bush Has Modernized Medicare And Provided More Than 40 Million Americans With Better Access To Prescription Drugs

President Bush has helped Americans receive the health care they need at a price they can afford, while empowering beneficiaries to make their own decisions to best meet their health needs. The President proposed broad Medicare reforms, and Congress responded by passing the historic Medicare Prescription Drug, Improvement, and Modernization Act of 2003, which has provided the most significant reforms to the Medicare program in nearly 40 years – providing preventive care, offering Medicare beneficiaries market-based choices, and giving seniors and people with disabilities better access to the prescription drugs they need.

President Bush Reformed Medicare To Add A Prescription Drug Benefit, Give Beneficiaries More Private Plan Choices, And Add Preventive Services

These programs have been a great success for our Nation's Medicare beneficiaries. The Medicare prescription drug benefit has provided more than 40 million Americans – including nearly 10 million low-income beneficiaries – with better access to prescription drugs. More than 25 million are in the new Part D program, either through a stand-alone drug plan or through a Medicare Advantage drug plan, in which beneficiaries receive benefits through private health insurance. In addition, 6.7 million have Medicare-subsidized retiree coverage through their employer or union plan, while 7.5 million have other creditable drug coverage.

Nearly 10 million people, more than 20 percent of Medicare beneficiaries, are enrolled in Medicare Advantage and receive their comprehensive Medicare benefits through a private plan option. Beneficiary satisfaction rates in these plans are high, and most beneficiaries receive additional value, including reduced premiums, lower cost sharing, and extra benefits. Making this program stable and predictable was one of the President's goals, and as a result of the changes made in 2003, almost every county in America has a private plan choice, many with zero premiums.

The President modernized Medicare to focus more on preventive care. Part of modern, effective health care is recognizing that if diseases are caught early, effective treatment is more likely, increasing the potential to reduce both cost and suffering. Every beneficiary entering Medicare who elects Part B is now eligible for a "Welcome to Medicare" exam within the first twelve months of coverage. Medicare is now covering cardiovascular blood screenings, diabetes screening, ultrasound screenings for aneurysms, and smoking cessation counseling that can catch illnesses like diabetes and heart disease.

Prescription drug coverage helps beneficiaries in four important ways:

1. **Medicare drug coverage helps all beneficiaries pay for prescription drugs, no matter how they paid before.** The average value of the standard Part D benefit in 2008 was roughly $1,100. Private employers receive incentives to continue to provide drug coverage to their retirees.

2. **Medicare drug coverage offers many choices for beneficiaries.** Beneficiaries can choose from a number of private plans to find the one that best serves them – and plan providers are competing for beneficiaries' business. That means beneficiaries can save more and get the coverage they want.

3. **Beneficiaries who have the highest drug costs receive extra help.** Beneficiaries with the standard benefit who enter the coverage gap will already have received an average benefit value totaling about $1,700 in 2008 because of Part D benefit. The coverage gap is the temporary limit on what most plans will cover for prescription drugs. For those with very high costs, Medicare will pick up as much as 95 percent of all prescription costs, for example, once they spend $4,050 of their own money in 2008.

4. **Medicare is providing extra help to low-income beneficiaries.** In 2008, approximately 38 percent of beneficiaries enrolled in a prescription drug plan or Medicare Advantage prescription drug plan are receiving prescription drug coverage that includes little or no premiums, low deductibles, and no gaps in coverage. On average, Medicare will pay for more than 95 percent of the costs of prescription drugs for low-income beneficiaries.

Competition Is Helping To Reduce Medical Costs For Consumers And Taxpayers

Private sector competition has resulted in more innovation and flexibility in coverage. Under President Bush's Medicare Part D policy, private health plans compete by providing better coverage at affordable prices – helping to control the costs of Medicare by marketplace competition, not government price-setting.

➤ **The estimated costs of this program to taxpayers have declined nearly 38 percent since enactment.** Costs to taxpayers are projected to be about $240 billion lower than originally estimated for 2004-2013. From 2006 to 2013, States are expected to spend about $25 billion less than originally projected.

➤ **In addition to the government savings, beneficiaries are also spending less than originally estimated.** The average premium that beneficiaries paid for a standard prescription drug benefit in 2008 was roughly $25 per month, nearly 40 percent lower than original estimates.

Beneficiaries Are Satisfied With Medicare Prescription Drug Coverage

Overall satisfaction is very high. Public opinion surveys in 2007 indicate satisfaction rates of over 85 percent.
- 87 percent – *Wall Street Journal*/Harris Interactive (December 2007)
- 86 percent – VCR Research/Medicare Rx Education Network (November 2007)
- 89 percent – KRC for *Medicare Today* (October 2007)

According to the 2008 *Medicare Today* Survey:
- 80 percent said that their plan covers all medicines.
- 84 percent indicated that their total out-of-pocket costs are reasonable.
- 95 percent responded that their plan was convenient to use.
- 86 percent said that their co-payments and premiums were affordable.

President Bush Has Improved How We Address Human Need Through Faith-Based And Community Initiatives

"[T]he Administration has upheld its promise to treat community and faith-based organizations as trusted partners.... You've helped revolutionize the way government addresses the greatest challenges facing our society."

– President George W. Bush, 6/26/08

The Mentoring Children of Prisoners (MCP) program has exceeded its goal of securing mentor matches for 100,000 children with incarcerated parents. Today, more than 110,000 children of prisoners have been matched with a caring mentor who can provide the consistent guidance and support these children need to succeed in life.

The Faith-Based and Community Initiative Has Revolutionized The Way Our Government Addresses The Greatest Challenges Facing Our Society

- President Bush created the Faith-Based and Community Initiative with his first Executive Order to lead a determined attack on need in partnerships with frontline nonprofits and to ensure faith-based organizations were welcomed as equal allies in this work. The Initiative has transformed the way government addresses human need and increased its effectiveness by:
  o Expanding partnerships with local nonprofits to battle poverty, disease and other ills.
  o Securing a "level playing field" for faith-based organizations and establishing clear, constitutional guidelines for their use of public funds.
- To strengthen America's "armies of compassion," the Initiative:
  o Trained more than 150,000 social entrepreneurs on how to increase the impact of their work.
  o Supported amendments to the tax code that provide greater incentives for charitable giving and activities.
  o Established the Compassion Capital Fund to provide grants and training designed to increase the effectiveness of grassroots nonprofits.

The Faith-Based And Community Initiative Joined With The Armies Of Compassion To Wage A Determined Attack On Need

- **Access to Recovery (ATR) program:** Provided nearly 270,000 recovering addicts with vouchers that enabled them to choose from an expansive network of faith-based and other community organizations (FBCOs) for the clinical and supportive services that best met their individual needs. Thousands of participating FBCOs helped produce results that outperform many national programs on multiple measures.
- **The President's Prisoner Re-entry Initiative:** Links returning nonviolent offenders with FBCOs that help them find work and avoid relapse into criminal activity. Participants' rate of re-arrest within one year of release is 15 percent, less than half the national average.
- **Disadvantaged Students:** More than 515,000 children received after-school tutoring annually through Supplemental Educational Service providers, including FBCO partners.
- **Community Health Services:** The President's Community Health Center Initiative exceeded its goal of creating or expanding 1,200 community-based health centers, many of which are operated by FBCO grantees. The number of low-income individuals receiving medical services from these centers annually has increased by 5.8 million since 2001.
- **Homelessness:** Federal partnerships with FBCOs have been greatly expanded to combat homelessness, contributing to a nearly 30 percent reduction in chronic homelessness (approximately 50,000 individuals) from 2005 to 2007. The estimated number of homeless veterans was cut by nearly 40 percent from 2001 to 2007.
- **Global Health:** In FY 2007 alone, 87 percent of partners in the President's Emergency Plan for AIDS Relief (PEPFAR) were local organizations, mostly faith-based and community groups. The latest results show that PEPFAR now supports life-saving treatment for more than 2 million people worldwide.

The Faith-Based And Community Initiative Built A Powerful Network Of Public-Private Partnerships To Address Need

- Last year, the Federal government awarded direct, competitive grants to more than 19,000 FBCOs. Of those, more than 3,200 grants, totaling more than $2.2 billion, were awarded to faith-based organizations.
- The President's vision inspired State governments to develop their own FBCI programs. Today, 36 governors (19 Democrats and 17 Republicans) and more than 70 mayors of both parties have their own Faith-Based and Community Initiative offices and/or liaisons.

USA Freedom Corps: Strengthening Service to Meet Community Needs

- **Following 9/11, President George W. Bush called on all Americans to serve their communities, their Nation, and their world.** In his 2002 State of the Union Address, he announced the creation of USA Freedom Corps to connect Americans with more opportunities to serve their country and to foster a culture of citizenship, responsibility, and service.

- **Nearly 61 million Americans have answered the President's Call to Service by volunteering.** These volunteers are helping feed the hungry, house the homeless, aid the addicted, mentor at-risk youth, and offer critical care to those in need at home and around the world.

USA Freedom Corps Is Helping Americans Answer The President's Call To Service By Strengthening National Service Programs

- **Citizen Corps**, created by President Bush following 9/11 to build a culture of preparedness, now has nearly one million volunteers nationwide, and their efforts reach more than three-quarters of the American people. Citizen Corps fosters collaboration among government and civic leaders to achieve broader participation in disaster preparedness and response.

- **Volunteers for Prosperity**, also created by President Bush, mobilized more than 43,000 doctors, teachers, engineers, and other skilled Americans this year to address critical needs abroad. The program matches skilled American professionals with service opportunities in the developing world. Both Citizen Corps and Volunteers for Prosperity have proven to be effective, and President Bush calls on Congress to make these programs permanent.

- **Peace Corps** has been provided its highest level of funding in history under President Bush. The Peace Corps has opened or re-opened programs in 13 countries. It currently supports about 8,000 Americans who commit to serve two years in communities overseas.

- **AmeriCorps** provides opportunities for more than 74,000 people to serve their fellow Americans.

- **Senior Corps** connected approximately 500,000 older Americans with opportunities to serve their communities and country through Retired and Senior Volunteer Program (RSVP), Senior Companions, and Foster Grandparents programs. Last year, Senior Corps members provided approximately 116 million hours of service.

- **Learn and Serve America** supported 1,700 grantees for service-learning programs in schools last year alone, engaging more than 1.4 million students from kindergarten through college in nearly 28 million hours of service.

- **Take Pride in America** was re-launched at the U.S. Department of the Interior and is supporting more than 400,000 skilled volunteers through meaningful service opportunities preserving America's public lands and National Parks.

USA Freedom Corp's website www.volunteer.gov created a volunteer network that has become the Nation's largest clearinghouse of volunteer opportunities. Volunteer.gov offers more than four million volunteer opportunities, both in the United States and abroad.

- **USA Freedom Corps plays a vital role in the aftermath of disasters like Hurricanes Gustav and Katrina, helping to link more than 1.1 million volunteers with opportunities to assist with relief efforts.** As part of this effort, more than 93,000 participants in national service programs have given 3.5 million hours of service in response to Katrina. National service participants from AmeriCorps and Senior Corps have supported or managed more than 262,000 community volunteers. Americans have also donated more than $3.5 billion to help the recovery and rebuilding effort.

- **President Bush has personally recognized more than 660 outstanding volunteers throughout the United States with the President's Volunteer Service Award.** In total, more than 1.1 million Americans have received the President's Volunteer Service Award, in recognition of their time spent in service to others. Today the President welcomed to the White House many of the volunteers he has honored to celebrate their achievements and thank them once again for their service.

- **President Bush created the President's Council on Service and Civic Participation, which launched a "Pro Bono Challenge" six months ago and has secured corporate pledges totaling more than $400 million.** The Council is charged with promoting volunteerism and advancing corporate social responsibility. It brings together leaders from the worlds of business, entertainment, sports, education, government, nonprofits, and media to echo President Bush's Call to Service. The national "Pro Bono Challenge" encourages companies to promote skills-based volunteering by their employees to help build the capacity of nonprofits meeting community needs.

- **Today USA Freedom Corps issued a report, "Answering the Call to Service," a comprehensive look at the work of the initiative to improve communities and change lives over nearly seven years under the President's leadership.** The report details the response from the millions of individuals who have answered the President's Call to Service and used their power and energy to affect communities across America. To view the report, visit www.volunteer.gov.

Diversifying Our Energy Supply And Confronting Climate Change

President Bush Has Strengthened America's Energy Security And Taken Constructive Steps To Confront Climate Change

President Bush has taken a reasoned, balanced approach to the serious challenges of energy security and climate change. The President supports a climate change policy that takes advantage of new clean energy technologies; increases our use of alternative fuels; works towards an international agreement that will slow, stop, and eventually reverse the growth of greenhouse gases; and includes binding commitments from all major economies.

➤ **Since President Bush took office, the Federal Government has invested more than $44 billion for climate-change and energy security programs, including more than $22 billion for technology research, development, and demonstration.** Technology funding for 2008 alone exceeded $4 billion.

➤ **President Bush signed laws giving the Department of Energy the authority to provide more than $67 billion in loans and guarantees to help support innovative energy projects to reduce greenhouse gases and air pollution and to retool auto plants to produce more efficient vehicles.** Under the new authority, up to $42.5 billion has been made available for innovative technology loan guarantees, of which $18.5 billion in loan guarantees will support construction of new nuclear plants and reduce interest costs for building plants. A significant portion of the more than $4 billion spent annually on Farm Bill conservation programs will also go to efforts to sequester greenhouse gases.

➤ **President Bush called for and signed new Federal mandates and his Administration has worked with States to adopt mandatory programs cutting emissions and improving energy security in every major sector.** The new Federal mandates will reduce greenhouse gas emissions billions of tons below projections.

➤ **The President led a global agreement that will dramatically cut emissions of a potent greenhouse gas by more than what the Kyoto Protocol might achieve.**

➤ **In April 2008, the President announced a new national goal to stop the growth in United States greenhouse gas emissions by 2025 and reverse it thereafter.** This would prevent billions of metric tons of greenhouse gas emissions from entering the atmosphere.

➤ **From 2002 to 2006, United States greenhouse gas emissions increased by only 1.9 percent, while the economy grew 12.6 percent.** In 2002, President Bush set a national goal to reduce greenhouse gas intensity 18 percent by 2012. We are well on track to meet or exceed that goal.

➤ **This year, President Bush removed the executive prohibition on offshore exploration for oil and gas.** In addition, the President successfully pressured Congress to remove its ban on offshore exploration and took steps to increase domestic oil exploration to reduce our dependence on foreign oil.

The United States Is Reducing Emissions And Dependence On Oil By Increasing The Use Of Renewable Fuels And Improving Energy Efficiency

Ethanol production has quadrupled from 1.6 billion gallons in 2000 to an estimated 6.5 billion gallons in 2007. In 2005, the United States became the world's leading ethanol producer, and last year, the United States accounted for nearly half of worldwide ethanol production.

The Administration has dedicated more than $1 billion to advance cellulosic ethanol made from switchgrass, wood chips, and other non-food sources. Since the President took office, the projected cost of cellulosic ethanol has dropped by more than 60 percent.

Last year, the United States produced about 490 million gallons of biodiesel – up 96 percent from 2006. Today, there are more than 968 biodiesel fueling stations, and hundreds of fleet operators use biodiesel to fuel their trucks. Every year, more Americans are realizing the benefits of biodiesel, which can be produced from soybeans and other vegetable oils, including waste products like recycled cooking grease.

Over the last five years, the Federal Government has invested approximately $1.2 billion in hydrogen research and development to help bring hydrogen fuel cell vehicles to market. These vehicles use no gasoline at all and emit clean, pure water.

In 2007, President Bush signed the Energy Independence and Security Act (EISA), which responded to his "Twenty in Ten" challenge to expand alternative fuels and improve vehicle fuel economy. Although the President's proposed alternative fuel standard would have gone further and faster than this legislation, EISA represents a major step forward in expanding the production of renewable fuels, reducing our dependence on oil, and confronting global climate change.

- The Renewable Fuels Mandate will require nearly five times as much renewable fuel as previous law – requiring fuel producers to supply at least 36 billion gallons of renewable fuel in the year 2022.
- The Vehicle Fuel Economy Mandate specifies a national mandatory fuel economy standard of 35 miles per gallon by 2020, which will save billions of gallons of fuel and increase fuel economy by 40 percent from their current levels.
- Taken together, according to the Energy Information Administration forecast, these two requirements will contribute to reducing our dependence on foreign oil from 58.2 percent in 2007 to 54.8 percent in 2018.

Additionally, EISA advances other energy efficiency initiatives:
- The Lighting Efficiency Mandate will phase out the use of standard incandescent light bulbs by 2014 and improve lighting efficiency by more than 70 percent by 2020.
- The Appliance Efficiency Mandates will require a fully updated series of new national standards in five years.
- The Federal Government Operations Mandate will reduce the energy intensity of Federal Government facilities 30 percent by 2015 and increase use of renewable fuel by 20 percent compared to 2003 levels, codifying two goals of President Bush's Executive Order 13423 issued in January 2007. Additionally, the law requires that all new Federal buildings be carbon-neutral in operations by 2030.

The United States Is Reducing Dependence On Fossil Fuels By Replacing Them With Alternative Energy Sources To Power Our Homes And Workplaces

Since 2001, the United States has increased wind energy production by more than 400 percent. Last year, more than 20 percent of new electrical generating capacity added in the United States came from wind – up from just three percent a few years ago. Wind power now supplies one percent of the United States' electricity.

Between 2000 and 2007, the United States' solar energy capacity doubled – and last year, the United States' solar installations grew by more than 32 percent.

The Administration also launched the Nuclear Power 2010 program and other significant efforts that helped encourage industry to submit 17 applications for 26 new nuclear reactors in the United States.

- **The Administration invested more than $300 million in research and development of nuclear energy technologies in 2007 alone.**

The Administration Is Leading The Way Toward An International Agreement To Slow, Stop, And Reverse The Growth Of Greenhouse Gases

- ➤ **The Administration launched an innovative series of meetings with the world's major economies that use the most energy and emit the most greenhouse gases.** Since President Bush launched the Major Economies Meeting

(MEM) in May 2007 there has been growing international agreement that, to be effective, a global framework will require commitments from all major economies – both industrialized and emerging – to take actions to reduce emissions.

The United States Has Formed International Partnerships To Pursue Clean And Renewable Energy Options

President Bush has proposed $2 billion over the next three years to create an international Clean Technology Fund to address the growing problem of accelerating greenhouse gas emissions in major developing countries. With contributions from Australia, Japan, the U.K., and other countries, this fund will accelerate the deployment of cleaner, more efficient technologies in developing nations with large greenhouse gas emissions.

The United States launched technology programs, such as the Global Nuclear Energy Partnership, with 21 partners so far, to pursue technology breakthroughs to support the long-term expansion of clean, safe, proliferation-resistant nuclear power here and around the world – and develop better ways to deal with the waste. The United States is leading similar technology partnerships on carbon capture and storage, hydrogen, fusion, renewable energy, energy efficiency, and bio-fuels.

The United States has also launched a series of practical international partnerships to cut emissions, improve energy security, and foster sustainable development. These include the Asia Pacific Partnership on Clean Development and Climate Change (with Australia, Canada, China, India, Korea, and Japan), the Methane to Markets Partnership (with 20 nations), and work on tropical forest conservation and stopping illegal logging.

The United States has led the way in proposing in WTO Doha negotiations an agreement to eliminate tariffs and non-tariff barriers on environmental goods and services, including technologies that will make a significant contribution to greenhouse gas reduction and improved energy security.

President Bush Has Advanced Cooperative Conservation And Protected The Environment

Because Of The President's Efforts To Encourage Cooperative Conservation, Innovation, And New Technologies, America's Air Is Cleaner, Our Water Is Purer, And Our Natural Resources Are Better Protected

"America's greatness is not measured by material wealth alone; it's measured by how we manage and care for all that we have been given. We're people united by our belief that we must be good stewards of our environment."

– President George W. Bush, 10/20/07

Encouraged And Promoted Conservation Of Our Natural Resources

- Instituted policies that helped reduce air pollution by 12 percent from 2001 to 2007 and adopted new policies that will produce even deeper reductions. Established stringent air quality standards and adopted rules that will cut hazardous industrial emissions and will cut power plant emissions by nearly 70 percent and diesel engine emissions by more than 90 percent.
- Signed an Executive Order making cooperative conservation the national policy of the United States and directed Federal agencies to implement resource laws cooperatively with State, local and tribal governments, and the public.
- Cleared dry brush and dead trees and thinned overstocked forests on 27 million acres of forest and range lands through the Healthy Forest Initiative to help prevent catastrophic wildfires, assist in executing core components of the National Fire Plan, and restore these ecosystems to healthy, natural conditions.
- Restored, improved, or protected more than 3 million acres of wetlands, improving water quality and creating wildlife habitats, largely through farm bill conservation programs, the North American Wetlands Conservation Act, and other cooperative conservation efforts. Set a new goal to protect, improve, and restore another 4 million acres.
- Expanded Federal tax incentives to encourage landowners to donate their property for conservation purposes. Strengthened and expanded the Conservation Reserve Program through which we are helping ranchers and farmers restore grassland habitats on their land.
- Created 15 new National Wildlife Refuges and emphasized recovery goals under the Endangered Species Act.
    - Efforts to conserve the populations of both the bald eagle and the Yellowstone grizzly bear have led to their recovery and removal from the Endangered Species List.
    - The Administration listed the polar bear as a threatened species under the Endangered Species Act and has further developed a polar bear action plan to help protect the species.
- Facilitated an agreement among Arizona, California, Colorado, Nevada, New Mexico, Utah, and Wyoming on water allocation during shortages and surpluses. This two-year effort enables the Department of the Interior to better manage Federal reservoirs while meeting the water needs of the seven States.
- Advanced a series of highly complex, regional resource conservation and management initiatives in partnership with the States, including with regard to the Everglades, Gulf of Mexico, Great Lakes, Pacific Coast, Columbia River, and Klamath River Basin.

Preserved Our National Parks And Community Heritage

- Announced the National Park Centennial Initiative in 2006, which increased funding to hire more park rangers, repair buildings, improve natural landscapes, and engage more children as junior rangers – an initiative Mrs. Laura Bush has actively supported and promoted.
- Performed more than $1 billion in assessments and clean-ups where necessary on more than 10,000 abandoned and contaminated industrial sites through the Brownfields Program.
- Provided nearly $17 million in grants through the Preserve America Initiative to advance efforts to protect our cultural and natural heritage in all 50 States: awarded more than 220 Preserve America grants and recognized more than 700 communities as Preserve America Communities. Mrs. Bush has also actively supported and promoted this initiative.
- Signed an Executive Order to facilitate the expansion and enhancement of hunting opportunities and the management of game species and their habitat.

Preserved Our Oceans

- Accomplished conservation in marine environments over the last eight years on par with what we've achieved on land over the past 100.
- Released an Ocean Action Plan in 2004 and created the first ever Cabinet Committee on Ocean Policy. All 88 actions recommended in the Ocean Action Plan have been met or are on track, making our oceans' coasts and Great Lakes cleaner, healthier, and more productive.
- Designated nearly 140,000 square miles of coral reef ecosystems and surrounding waters in the Northwestern Hawaiian Islands, which contains more than 7,000 species, many of which are found nowhere else on earth, as the Papahānaumokuākea Marine National Monument – giving the area our Nation's highest form of marine environmental protection.
- Designated three areas of the Pacific Ocean, covering more than 195,500 square miles, as marine national monuments: the Mariana, Pacific Remote Islands, and Rose Atoll Marine National Monuments.
- Announced the expansion of the Monterey Bay National Marine Sanctuary by 775 square miles to include the Davidson Sea Mount.
- Protected our oceans by taking action to end overfishing and conserve habitats.
- Increased funding for the National Oceanic Atmospheric Administration by $770 million since he took office.

Protected Fish And Birds

- Directed Secretary of State Condoleezza Rice, in consultation with Secretary of Commerce Carlos Gutierrez, to strengthen efforts to protect sustainable fisheries and call for an end to destructive fishing practices on the high seas. In December 2006, in an effort spearheaded by the United States, the United Nations passed a resolution to help protect fish stocks and marine habitats from destructive fishing practices.
- Signed an Executive Order to conserve as gamefish two of America's most popular recreational fish – striped bass and red drum – for the recreational, economic, and environmental benefit of present and future generations.
- Signed the Magnuson-Stevens Fishery Conservation and Management Reauthorization Act of 2006 and reaffirmed our commitment to protect America's fisheries and keep our commercial and recreational fishing communities strong.
- Preserved and restored stopover habitat for migratory birds in the United States through the Migratory Bird Initiative and put forth an innovative policy called "recovery credit trading," which provides a new tool to help in habitat conservation.

Advancing Stem Cell Research In Ethical, Responsible Ways

Research Has Justified President Bush's Commitment To Support Responsible Research On Pluripotent Stem Cells

President Bush's Balanced Stem Cell Policies Are Helping Advance Science And Ethics Together

In 2001, President Bush announced a balanced approach to stem cell research that would allow Federal funding for research using existing embryonic stem cell lines. This policy allowed the Federal government to support research on dozens of existing stem cell lines without sanctioning or encouraging the destruction of additional human embryos.

President Bush is the first President to provide Federal funding for human embryonic stem cell research. Since 2001, the Administration has made more than $170 million available for research on stem cell lines derived from human embryos that had already been destroyed. In addition, the Administration has provided nearly $3.7 billion for research on all forms of stem cells, including those from adult and other non-embryonic sources.

The President opposes any attempt to compel American taxpayers to pay for research that relies on the intentional destruction of human embryos. He believes that by enacting appropriate policy safeguards while encouraging the development of new scientific techniques, it is possible to advance science and medicine without violating moral principles.

President Bush has encouraged scientific advancement of stem cell research within ethical boundaries by avoiding techniques that destroy life, while vigorously supporting alternative approaches. Research indicates that pluripotent stem cells – those that have the potential to develop into nearly all the cell types and tissues in the body – can be derived without using or harming embryos. The President has long supported these non-embryonic techniques, and there has been exciting progress over the past couple of years:
- In November 2007, several new studies showed the potential of reprogramming adult cells, such as skin cells, to make them function like embryonic stem cells.
- Since then, researchers have increasingly used these ethically uncontroversial cells in the same kinds of research for which embryonic stem cells had been used, and numerous published studies have now shown their usefulness.
- As of October 2008, it is estimated that more than 800 labs are now using these new uncontroversial cells.

The President has acted to strengthen our Nation's commitment to conduct research on pluripotent stem cells. In June 2007, he signed an Executive Order to expand support for these non-destructive research methods and make it more likely that exciting advances in this area will continue. The Order:
- Invited scientists to work with the National Institutes of Health (NIH) to add new ethically derived, human pluripotent stem cell lines to the list of those eligible for Federal funding.
- Directed the Department of Health and Human Services and the NIH to ensure that any human pluripotent stem cell lines produced in ways that do not create, destroy, or harm human embryos will be eligible for Federal funding.
- Expanded the NIH's Embryonic Stem Cell Registry to include all types of ethically produced human pluripotent stem cells. The NIH is planning to add to the Registry new pluripotent stem cell lines that are not derived from embryos.
- Renamed the registry the Pluripotent Stem Cell Registry – so that it reflects what the stem cells can do, instead of where they come from.

In September 2007, the NIH implemented the President's Executive Order. The plan contained a number of new or accelerated activities, including two fresh funding streams to stimulate research on human pluripotent stem cells derived from non-embryonic sources:
- The NIH Stem Cell Task Force developed a pair of program announcements to solicit grant applications for research on human pluripotent stem cells derived from non-embryonic sources.

- In addition, the Stem Cell Task Force developed another funding opportunity to rapidly stimulate research in human pluripotent stem cells from non-embryonic sources. This initiative awarded additional funding to NIH-supported researchers already working in stem cell research to supplement certain areas of their work that are of particular interest to NIH.

In April 2008, the Department of Defense announced the creation of the Armed Forces Institute for Regenerative Medicine (AFIRM), a new partnership among the Federal government, universities, and private companies. Regenerative medicine is a promising new field focused on the repair and replacement of tissues and organs, which has been made possible in part by progress in stem cell research. The Center's goal is to take ethical stem cell-based innovations out of the lab and make them a life-improving reality for our wounded warriors and other Americans.

In his 2008 State of the Union Address, President Bush called on Congress to pass legislation that bans unethical practices such as the buying, selling, patenting, or cloning of human life.

Judges Who Honor The Constitution

President Bush Has Appointed Judges Who Do Not Legislate From The Bench

Of President Bush's judicial nominees, the Senate has confirmed **61** Circuit Court judges and **261** District Court judges (as of October 6, 2008). Today more than one-third of all Federal judges have been appointed by him – and these men and women are jurists of the highest caliber with an abiding belief in the sanctity of our Constitution.

Judges Matter To Every American, And The Belief In Judicial Restraint Is Shared By The Vast Majority Of Our Nation

The judicial branch has the potential to wield enormous power. It is the only branch of government whose officers are unelected. That means the judges appointed to the Federal bench should exercise their power prudently, cautiously, and conservatively. Judges can have a profound impact on the daily lives of every citizen.

➢ **The proper role of judges is to apply the laws as written, and not to advance their own agendas.** Eight years ago when President Bush was seeking the presidency, he said America needed judges who believed that the Constitution means what it says. So when he took office, he promised the American people that his Administration would seek out judicial nominees who follow that philosophy. He has kept that pledge.

President Bush Has Appointed To The Supreme Court Two Jurists Of Decency, Integrity, And Good Judgment

President Bush's judicial philosophy is demonstrated most clearly by the outstanding judges he has appointed to the bench. America is particularly well served by President Bush's appointments to the Supreme Court.

➢ **Chief Justice John Roberts:** He received his bachelor's degree from Harvard in just three years and was managing editor of the Harvard Law Review. He clerked for the Chief Justice whom he would later replace, William H. Rehnquist. Chief Justice Roberts' philosophy is: "Judges are like umpires. Umpires don't make the rules; they apply them ... It is a limited role. Nobody ever went to a ball game to see the umpire."

➢ **Justice Samuel Alito:** He graduated from Princeton and Yale Law School, served in Ronald Reagan's Justice Department, was U.S. Attorney for the District of New Jersey, and served as judge for the United States Court of Appeals for the Third Circuit. When the President nominated him, this good man was hailed by Democrats and Republicans alike for his keen mind and impeccable credentials.

Mrs. Laura Bush's Leadership
First Lady's Work Advances President Bush's Agenda At Home And Abroad

Mrs. Laura Bush is an effective ambassador on important issues for the President and our Nation. As First Lady, she traveled domestically to all 50 States and internationally to more than 75 countries. A leading advocate for literacy, Mrs. Bush has championed the power of education to foster healthy families and communities, advance opportunity for young people, and promote human rights worldwide, particularly for women and children.

Mrs. Bush Is Actively Involved In Supporting The President's Global Diplomatic Efforts

The United States is working with the international community to promote peace, stability, and reconstruction in Afghanistan. In 2001, fewer than a million Afghan children were in school – all of them boys. Today, more than six million Afghan children are in school – about a third of them girls. Since the fall of the Taliban, Afghanistan's infant-mortality rate has been reduced by almost 25 percent, and 85 percent of Afghans now have access to basic healthcare.

➢ **Mrs. Bush made three trips to Afghanistan to underscore the United States' commitment to the country's rebuilding and development.** In 2001, President Bush turned the microphone over to Mrs. Bush for the weekly radio address, where she spoke out about the oppression of women and children under the Taliban. Since 2001, Mrs. Bush has routinely met with Afghan students, teachers, parliamentarians, and judges during their visits to the United States for education and training.

➢ **In June 2008, Mrs. Bush traveled to Bamiyan and met with the province's governor Habiba Sarabi, Afghanistan's first and only woman governor.** Governor Sarabi's appointment in 2005 was a historic milestone in the advancement of Afghan women. Mrs. Bush also met with women entrepreneurs and visited the Bamiyan Regional Police Training Center where she met with several women police officers.

➢ **As Honorary Chair of the U.S.-Afghan Women's Council, Mrs. Bush helps inspire both public and private partnerships to support Afghanistan.** The Council has implemented over 30 initiatives in the areas of economic empowerment, education, political participation, health, and children's issues totaling approximately $70 million.

➢ **In Paris, on June 12, 2008, Mrs. Bush addressed the International Conference in Support of Afghanistan, urging the international community to offer the political and economic assistance Afghanistan needs to recover from decades of war and oppression.** Following her third historic visit to Afghanistan, her remarks reiterated the President's commitment to aid the men, women, and children of Afghanistan as they rebuild their country. At the conference, Mrs. Bush announced a $10.2 billion pledge for U.S. assistance to Afghanistan. Total U.S. humanitarian, development, and security assistance appropriated since 2001 is more than $26 billion.

Mrs. Bush actively supports the people of Burma as they struggle to free themselves from the regime's tyranny.

➢ **The United States has called on the international community to support the people of Burma in bringing peaceful change to their country.** Mrs. Bush hosted a roundtable at the United Nations Headquarters in 2006 to draw attention in the international community to human rights problems in Burma. In subsequent editorials, interviews, and public statements, she has continued to cast the spotlight on the plight of the Burmese people.

➢ **As part of her ongoing call to the international community to assist the Burmese people in their struggle for democracy and human rights, Mrs. Bush traveled to the Thai-Burma border.** In August 2008, Mrs. Bush visited the Mae La refugee camp and the Mae Tao medical clinic to learn first-hand of the refugees' plight and their desire for education and freedom. Mae La, the largest of nine camps along the western Thailand border, shelters over 35,000 refugees, and provides free health care to hundreds of refugees each day.

➢ **Mrs. Bush has protested the violent crackdown of the ruling junta against peaceful protesters and the prolonged detainment of Aung San Suu Kyi, a Nobel Laureate and leader of Burma's freely-elected, pro-democratic party.** She has called on the regime to stop its terror campaigns against its own people; to release all political prisoners; to commit to a meaningful, unrestricted dialogue with opposition leaders; and to take steps to foster a democratic transition.

She has also called on the international community to refrain from purchasing Burmese gemstones, the revenue from which props up the repressive Burmese regime rather helping the people of Burma.

> **On May 5, 2008, Mrs. Bush held a press conference in the White House Press Briefing Room and called on the junta to allow unhindered access for international disaster experts and aid providers so that the Burmese people could receive the assistance they need in the wake of the devastating Cyclone Nargis.**

Mrs. Bush Is A Leading Advocate For Literacy And Education In The United States And Around The World

As Honorary Ambassador for the UN Literacy Decade, Mrs. Bush highlights the vital importance of literacy in addressing the challenges facing the developing world. In 2006, Mrs. Bush convened leaders from around the world for the White House Conference on Global Literacy. Her commitment inspired six subsequent regional conferences, which addressed specific regional literacy challenges, promoted concrete country support, and fostered regional cooperation. By investing in literacy and education, governments give their people freedom to improve their lives, their health, their communities, and their nations.

In support of the President's international education initiatives, Mrs. Bush promotes education for boys and girls throughout Africa and the world. The President's Africa Education Initiative (AEI) committed $600 million from FY 2002 through FY 2010 to increase access to quality basic education opportunities in Africa through scholarships, textbooks, and teacher training programs. AEI has awarded scholarships in 40 countries, trained more than 730,000 teachers, and provided 8.5 million textbooks and other learning materials. More than 34 million children have been helped by AEI to date. In 2007, the President and Mrs. Bush announced the Initiative for Expanded Education for the World's Poorest Children and committed an additional $525 million to provide greater access to quality basic education in six target countries and new after-school skills development programs.

Mrs. Bush supports education reforms that are closing the achievement gap. She has played an instrumental role in the success of the No Child Left Behind Act of 2001, helping ensure every child can reach his or her full potential. Drawing on her experience as a teacher, Mrs. Bush helped shape the Reading First program, which is putting proven methods of reading instruction in our Nation's classrooms to ensure every child is proficient by the fourth grade.

Announced by President Bush in his 2005 State of the Union Address, the *Helping America's Youth* initiative, led by Mrs. Bush, encourages Americans to engage in helping young people become healthy adults. This nationwide effort works to raise awareness about the challenges facing youth, particularly at-risk boys, and to motivate caring adults to connect with youth in three key areas: family, school, and community.

> **The initiative has developed resources for caring adults who want to help America's youth.** In October 2005, Mrs. Bush convened the White House Conference on Helping America's Youth at Howard University in Washington, D.C. with parents, civic leaders, faith-based and community service providers, educators, and experts to address problems facing America's youth and showcase successful solutions. Six regional conferences co-hosted by Mrs. Bush provided training sessions and an expert speaker series to give State and local participants best practices, successful program guidance, and lessons learned to apply to their work on behalf of young people in their communities.

> **The vital work of *Helping America's Youth* will continue through a Presidential Working Group.** The President signed an Executive Order on February 7, 2008, formally establishing the Interagency Working Group on Youth Programs, a coalition of Federal agencies that will continue their work to support communities and organizations working to help our Nation's youth.

As founder of the National Book Festival, Mrs. Bush encourages Americans to celebrate books and the joy of reading. Co-hosted annually by the Library of Congress and Mrs. Bush, this event brings up to 120,000 visitors each year to the National Mall to hear award-winning authors read excerpts from their latest books.

Mrs. Bush actively supports Gulf Coast rebuilding efforts. In 24 visits to the Gulf Coast, Mrs. Bush has helped drive school recovery efforts for the 1,121 schools damaged or destroyed by hurricanes. She continues to encourage Americans to volunteer their time to invest in the future of the Crescent City and entire region.

Mrs. Bush Champions Health Initiatives That Are Saving Lives And Healing Countries

Mrs. Bush has focused domestic and international attention on the President's Emergency Plan for AIDS Relief (PEPFAR), the President's Malaria Initiative (PMI), and global efforts for breast cancer awareness and research.

➤ **In visits to 12 of the 15 PEPFAR focus countries in Africa, Asia, and the Americas, Mrs. Bush has seen firsthand the success of this historic commitment to the fight against global HIV/AIDS.** President Bush announced PEPFAR in 2003 as a five-year, $15 billion initiative – then the largest international health initiative in history to fight a single disease. In July 2008, the President signed bipartisan legislation to reauthorize PEPFAR for up to $48 billion for five additional years and to expand its programs to continue to combat HIV/AIDS, tuberculosis, and malaria. From 2003-2008, this effort helped bring life-saving treatment to 2.1 million people and supported care for more than 10 million people around the world.

➤ **Mrs. Bush has helped mobilize public and private efforts to address malaria.** Over the course of five trips to Africa, she has visited 10 of the 15 countries aided by the President's Malaria Initiative (PMI). The President and Mrs. Bush hosted the 2006 White House Summit on Malaria, bringing together international experts to establish a united effort to combat this preventable disease.

➤ **The United States is working with countries in the Middle East, Europe, and the Americas to end breast cancer.** During visits to nine countries, Mrs. Bush has encouraged women to take charge of their health and emphasized the importance of screenings and early detection. In Saudi Arabia, the number of women receiving breast cancer screenings at the Abdullatif Cancer Screening Center increased almost fivefold since the partnership began in 2006.

***The Heart Truth* campaign has helped save tens of thousands of women's lives.** In 2008, Mrs. Bush marked her fifth anniversary as *The Heart Truth* ambassador. Mrs. Bush has traveled throughout the United States to talk with women and raise their awareness of the risks of heart disease. As a wife and mother, Mrs. Bush recognizes the urgency for women to commit to a lifestyle that promotes lifelong health, not only for every woman's own benefit but also for the benefit of their families and loved ones.

➤ **More women are aware that heart disease is their number one cause of death.** Today, 62 percent of women recognize that heart disease is the most common cause of death for women, up from only 34 percent in 2000.

➤ **Fewer women are dying of heart disease.** Heightened awareness is leading to action. The last six years saw the first decline in decades in the number of heart disease deaths in women. The yearly decrease in deaths from heart disease since 2000 amounts to 36,703 lives saved. *The Heart Truth* campaign is empowering American women to fight back against heart disease, which is often preventable.

Mrs. Bush Is Working To Safeguard America's Heritage, Protect Our National Parks, And Conserve Our Oceans

President and Mrs. Bush's leadership has helped ensure that our Nation's priceless intellectual and cultural artifacts, historic structures, and historic sites continue to be preserved for future generations to enjoy.

➤ **Mrs. Bush has instilled in the next generation a sense of stewardship and pride in our National Parks**. In her role as Honorary Chair of the National Park Foundation and through programs like Junior Rangers and First Bloom, Mrs. Bush is encouraging youth across the country to appreciate and protect our country's national treasures and natural resources.

➤ **The National Parks Centennial Initiative announced by President Bush and championed by Mrs. Bush will help ensure America's National Parks are on track for another century of conservation, preservation, and enjoyment.** Over the next 10 years, increased government investment and private philanthropy will fund significant improvements to our National Parks that will enhance family experiences in parks by adding visitor services and restoring historic and cultural sites for public enjoyment.

➢ **Established by Executive Order on March 3, 2003, the Preserve America Initiative encourages and supports community efforts to protect America's priceless cultural and natural heritage.** Mrs. Bush advocates for the Initiative's work to establish a greater shared knowledge of our Nation's past, strengthen regional identities and local pride, increase local participation in preserving the country's cultural and natural heritage assets, and support the economic vitality of our communities. To that end, more than 180 Preserve America grants have been awarded, totaling $12.7 million to date.

    • **On July 12, 2007, Mrs. Bush announced that President Bush sent proposed legislation to Congress for the Preserve America and Save America's Treasures Act.** If passed by the Congress, the Act will help ensure the government's continued ability to protect America's historic places, objects, and collections for many years to come.

➢ **Mrs. Bush has championed conservation and protection of our oceans and coastal resources.** Mrs. Bush announced the native Hawaiian name of the Northwestern Hawaiian Islands Marine National Monument, underscoring the importance of native Hawaiian culture and resource protection. She emphasized the important role of ocean literacy and education by designating the J. L. Scott Marine Education Center as a Coastal Ecosystem Learning Center. She also launched a Marine Debris Initiative to work with the private sector to clean up debris, educate the public about recycling and trash disposal, and work with our international partners to reduce the amount of marine debris entering the ocean.

www.ingramcontent.com/pod-product-compliance
Lightning Source LLC
Chambersburg PA
CBHW080627290526
45790CB00007B/2951

* 9 7 8 1 5 1 1 5 2 2 9 8 4 *